Kilimanjaro

A PHOTOGRAPHIC JOURNEY
TO THE ROOF OF AFRICA

TEXT BY MICHEL MOUSHABECK
PHOTOGRAPHY BY HILTRUD SCHULZ

INTERLINK BOOKS

This edition first published in 2011

INTERLINK BOOKS

An imprint of Interlink Publishing Group, Inc.

46 Crosby Street, Northampton, Massachusetts 01060

www.interlinkbooks.com

Text copyright © Michel S. Moushabeck, 2009, 2011

Photography copyright © Hiltrud Schulz, 2009, 2011

Map on page 54 courtesy of Zainab A. Ansell, director, Zara Tours

Colobus monkeys photo on page is courtesy of Jacquetta Megarry

Special thanks to Steven Schoenberg for his help in preparing the sheet music

LIBRARY OF CONGRESS CATALOGING-IN-PUBLICATION DATA

Moushabeck, Michel.

Kilimanjaro : a photographic journey to the roof of Africa / text by Michel Moushabeck ; photography by Hiltrud Schulz.

   p. cm.

Includes bibliographical references.

ISBN 978-1-56656-781-7 (hardcover)—ISBN 978-1-56656-753-4 (pbk.)

1. Kilimanjaro, Mount (Tanzania)—Description and travel. 2. Kilimanjaro, Mount (Tanzania)—Pictorial works. 3. Kilimanjaro, Mount (Tanzania)—History. 4. Kilimanjaro, Mount (Tanzania)—Environmental conditions. I. Schulz, Hiltrud. II. Title.

DT449.K4M67 2009

967.8'26—dc22   2009004388

Printed and bound in China

To request our 40-page full-color catalog, please e-mail us at info@interlinkbooks.com, call us toll-free at 1-800-238-LINK, or visit our website at www.interlinkbooks.com

For our climbing partners Jetta and Guri; for our guide Bruce, our assistant guides Constantin and Fortunatus, and our cook Faustin; for our porters Adam, Peter, Richard, Tungaraza, Charles, Dani, Hamis, Musa, and Athuman

Asante sana. Tunakupenda.
—MM & HS

CONTENTS

How It All Started

There, ahead, all he could see, as wide as all the world, great, high, and unbelievably white in the sun, was the square top of Kilimanjaro.
—Ernest Hemingway, *The Snows of Kilimanjaro*

It happened in the space of a fifteen-minute meeting at the London Book Fair. One minute I was asking author Jacquetta Megarry about the status of her manuscript *Kilimanjaro: Summit of Africa*, the climbing guide we were releasing later in the fall, and the next minute I found myself asking, "Will you take me with you?"

During the meeting Jacquetta explained that she had climbed and written about the three most popular Mount Kilimanjaro climbing routes (Marangu, Machame, and Rongai), but that in order to complete the manuscript she would need to climb and write about the fourth remaining route, Lemosho, the least traveled but most scenic, where you could see the mountain almost the entire way.

What had just happened? And what had come over me? I'd been feeling stressed with work, a bit rundown generally, but it never crossed my mind before to attempt to climb a high mountain, let alone Africa's highest. Sure, I love the outdoors and I enjoy hiking and camping, but climbing a 19,340 foot (5,895 meters) mountain in thin air is no cakewalk! Why would I want to do this? Was I really up for the challenge? And, worst of all, how could I explain to Hildi that we were no longer going to Lisbon for our summer vacation? Conventional wisdom would dictate that I should first try going up a 10,000-footer or a 15,000-footer, but it was too late now; the words had already departed from my lips and I was not about to back down.

"Are you serious?" Jacquetta blurted with a surprised look on her face. "I'm dead serious," I answered, suddenly realizing that I'd just dug myself a deeper hole. She then proceeded to ask me about my climbing experience, which mountains I'd climbed, the highest peaks I'd summited, on which continents, and so on—normal questions to ask someone who is about to become your expedition partner. Jacquetta has written numerous climbing and long-distance walking guides. She's been on many expeditions to the world's highest mountains, including Everest, Aconcagua, and others. She could tell immediately that I had no high-altitude mountain climbing experience, but she was impressed with the fact that last summer Hildi and I climbed Mount Washington, the highest mountain in the northeast. It's only 6,288 feet (1,917 meters), but climbing it is no small feat. Its terrain is arduous— rocky, steep, and cold—and it is known to have the world's highest recorded wind velocity at its peak (231 mph on April 12, 1934).

We talked about Kilimanjaro the entire time and our meeting ended without our having really discussed any of the outstanding issues for which it was intended. We tentatively set June 19th—only two months away—as our Tanzania meeting date. Jacquetta said she would get in touch with Harry Kikstra, author of *Everest: Summit of the World*, and owner/operator of 7summits.com, the adventure tour outfit that had organized her last Kilimanjaro research trip. We hugged and said goodbye, and as I walked away, Jacquetta yelled: "See you in Kili!" That's when it really hit me—it's actually happening! For a brief moment I was overcome with excitement, but then one thought occupied my mind for the rest of the day: how to break the news to Hildi.

Later that evening when Hildi called, she sensed right away that something was going on. I answered the phone with "Hey, honey," an expression I rarely use but which sometimes unconsciously slips out when I'm about to deliver news I know she doesn't want to hear. "How would you like to climb Mount Kilimanjaro in June?" I asked, sounding upbeat. There was silence on the line. "Did you hear what I said?" I asked again. "Yes, I heard what you said, but I don't understand. Why Kilimanjaro? What about our vacation?" She wasted no time reminding me that we had already planned our vacation; that we were going to Lisbon; that we only get *one* vacation a year; and that our weary bodies needed a break after this year's harsh New England winter and long working hours. Of course, I knew all this. For several weeks we'd talked about nothing else. We'd watched Wim Wenders' film *Lisbon Story*; we'd read accounts by Thomas Mann and Simone de Beauvoir and other illustrious travelers to this sensual city; and we'd listened for hours on end to the melancholic music of Madredeus and Mariza, the ambassador of Portuguese fado. Getting lost in Lisbon's narrow, cobbled backstreets, hanging around cafés doing nothing, and savoring the delights of Portuguese food and wine had become the subject of our daily dinner conversation over the past few months.

We spoke on the phone for a long time that evening. In the end, after hearing the excitement in my voice—or maybe it was getting late and she was just too tired—Hildi said: "Okay, I'll go with you." From that moment on, climbing Mount Kilimanjaro—Africa's highest peak and the world's tallest free-standing mountain—became the topic of not only our dinner conversation but *all* our conversations.

Mount Kilimanjaro at sunrise as seen from Shira Camp
(11,480 feet/3,500 meters)

The Preparation

If I am asked "what is the use of climbing this highest mountain?" I reply:
No use at all—no more use than kicking a football about, or dancing, or playing the
piano, or writing a poem, or painting a picture.
—Mountaineer Francis Younghusband, 1913

Back at home in Massachusetts, an e-mail from Jacquetta was awaiting my arrival. With the words "Are you serious?" in the subject line, she gave us all the details of the trip and confirmed that all the arrangements had been made through Harry Kikstra at 7summits.com, but she wanted to make sure one last time that we were still on board before paying any deposit. I reassured her in my reply and attached a copy of our flight itinerary. The next day she wrote back: "Since we are now climbing partners you should call me Jetta from here on."

Jetta is a hardy, headstrong, no-nonsense, Scottish woman of sixty. We've known each other for eight or so years but we had never been close friends. I'd bump into her every now and then at book fair parties in Frankfurt or London, and we'd discuss business matters via e-mail, but we'd never really had a face-to-face conversation that lasted more than a few minutes. From our brief encounters I'd gotten the impression that she was nice, reliable, and got things done. But what would she be like on the mountain? Was she the bossy type who would want to do things her way? The talkative type who would disrupt my serene encounter with nature? Would we enjoy camping and having dinner with her for eight nights in a row? I quickly stopped myself from worrying about such things. The one thing that mattered when choosing a climbing partner, I said to myself, is experience—that's what climbing gurus Jon Krakauer and Ed Viesturs tell you in their books—and Jetta had plenty of it.

We had now passed the point of no return: the flights had been booked and the expedition paid for. With only two months of planning, we had to move quickly to obtain visas to Tanzania, get the needed vaccinations, buy the necessary gear, and—most importantly—get in shape. We needed to devise a set of exercises to increase endurance, balance, and core strength, but, primarily, we needed to train the heart to pump more blood so that it didn't malfunction at high altitude. We settled on a two-hour daily exercise regimen that included one hour on the treadmill (the length of a *Sex in the City* episode), half an hour on the Stairmaster (time enough for a CNN news update), and the remaining time using different weight-lifting machines. On weekends, we concentrated on cardio activity that involved the large muscle groups; we went for long walks in the woods behind our house and we speed-hiked up little mountains in surrounding towns. After a sluggish start at the gym, we managed to get ourselves into a routine and gradually started to see the results of our toils—thanks to those TV monitors attached to the treadmills that keep your head preoccupied while your feet do the running. I even got into the habit of doing sit-ups early in the morning when I got up and again at night just before I went into bed, something I haven't done since my teenage years. While I can't brag about any signs of a six-pack—not even remotely—or any bulging biceps, I am proud of the fact that by the end of our eight-week stint, I could easily run on the treadmill, at the highest incline, for the duration of a *Law and Order* double-feature.

—

Our pre-travel consultation with Dr. Ann Markes, a specialist in travel medicine, was very helpful. She gave us valuable advice on a range of travel-related illnesses, from diarrhea to malaria to hypothermia and acute mountain sickness. Having climbed Kilimanjaro herself, she explained to us how to recognize symptoms of high-altitude pulmonary edema (HAPE), caused by the swelling of tissues in the lungs, and high-altitude cerebral edema (HACE), caused by swelling in the brain. She stressed the importance of immediate descent when complications relating to these two conditions arose, and warned us that these are the most serious illnesses a climber could face on the mountain and should not be taken lightly. What I found alarming was the fact that there isn't much one can do for prevention; these complications could happen to anyone, no matter how fit they were. I read all about them in accounts written by famous mountaineers and in books such as *Into Thin Air* and *No Shortcuts to the Top*, but when you are told of these dangers, to your face, by your doctor, it somehow has a different effect altogether. For the first time, I felt a little worried and I started to torment myself with "what if" questions. What if I were suffering from a severe headache, disorientation, and hallucinations, would I have the wits and the energy to make an immediate rush down the mountain? What if I got cerebral edema and experienced loss of vision, how would I find my way down to a lower camp? Seeing the worried look on my face, the doctor reassured us by telling us about her wonderful experience on Kilimanjaro, which helped put my mind slightly at ease.

Seated comfortably in her leather chair, with an opened laptop resting on her legs, Dr. Markes spent the last ten minutes of our visit talking about recommended immunizations. She scrolled down a checklist on her computer and asked us about the dates of any previous vaccinations. As it turned out, I needed almost all the ones on her list: yellow fever, hepatitis A, hepatitis B, polio, influenza, tetanus, and typhoid. The only one I remembered having when I was a teenager was chickenpox. With so many shots, I jokingly asked her if I were entitled to a volume discount. Next door, a nurse was ready to give us our first set of shots. Hildi went first while I sat there waiting with my eyes shut. When my turn came, I asked for all my shots to be given in my left arm so I could save my right one for my tennis game the next morning. A few minutes later, the nurse signed our yellow vaccination certificates and we were on our way. As we walked out of the doctor's office, I felt my head spinning, my left arm aching from multiple injections, and my right hand firmly clenching a wad of prescriptions the doctor had given us for "just-in-case" situations (anti-diarrhea pills, Diamox to help you cope with high altitude, malaria pills, etc. ...). I looked at Hildi and gave a sigh of relief. I was glad that all the medical stuff was over and done with.

—

We spent the next couple of weeks reading about Kilimanjaro. In books, on websites, and blogs, we read everything there was to read about the mountain: its history and its people, its climbing pioneers, its flora and fauna, its magic. Now we were ready to buy the clothing and equipment we needed to take with us. We prepared a list of "must-haves"—duffel bags, hiking boots, sleeping bags, poles, headlamps, warm socks, gloves, camera—and another list we called "nice-to-have," which included my favorite trail mix, pee bottles, a couple of novels, a wildlife guide, gaiters, binoculars, a tripod, and extra energy bars. Initially, I thought this was going be the easy part of the trip preparation. How wrong I was! With weight being such an important consideration, buying the proper gear became a research project in and of itself. From early on, we realized that in order to stay within our weight limit of around thirty pounds per duffel bag most of the items on the "nice-to-have" list would have to be excluded. My Swiss Army knife, an item I was keen on taking with me, would also have to be sacrificed. "Can you imagine how US airport security would react if they found a Palestinian with climbing gear *and* a Swiss Army knife?" I thought to myself. Homeland Security would think they'd caught a big fish. "Do you think they'd believe me if I said I was going mountain-climbing for fun?" I've heard so many horror stories about racial profiling, where Arab tourists suddenly were treated as terrorists, humiliated and harassed by airport security. I wasn't taking any chances; we'd invested so much in this trip and I wasn't about to let anything get in the way of our adventure.

Our visit to our local outdoors store started us off on the right track, but some decisions proved more difficult than others. Choosing among the twenty-five or so styles of headlamps was easy—we chose the cheapest—but deciding on the right sleeping bag was not. We agonized over the choice of down versus synthetic, 0° F (-18° C) versus -15° F (-26° C) sleeping bags. But since Lemosho is strictly a camping route—and I really hate being cold— we opted for the -15° F synthetic ones, a wise decision reinforced by a blogger's comment: "Down sleeping bags tend to be warmer but you're screwed if they get wet." We then bought the rest of the needed warm clothes; the camelbacks; the poles; the amazingly small, self-inflating sleeping mats, which no camper should go without; the sleeping bag thermal liner for the freezing cold summit night; and the most important item of all: biodegradable toilet paper. We packed it all up in our duffel bags on the day of our departure and, at the last minute, I slipped a couple of small packs of my favorite trail mix into my duffel pocket.

The Journey

Life without companionship is a life without purpose.
—Sir Wilfred Thesiger, *Arabian Sands*

It is funny how life works out," I told Hildi while waiting to check in for our flight at Boston's Logan International Airport, "If someone had said to me when I was much younger that at age 53 I would be climbing Mount Kilimanjaro, I wouldn't have believed them." At the check-in counter, as our duffel bags were being weighed, I could feel my heart beating with excitement. But even for someone who gets the itch to travel every few weeks, this was a completely different thrill, one that must have been embedded deep in my soul for some time. The mountain evoked in me romantic notions of adventure and discovery: I couldn't wait to find out what it was really like day by day, minute by minute, to traverse its dramatic landscapes and treacherous glaciers, and to reach its nearly 20,000-foot/6,000-meter-high peak.

Our overnight flight arrived at London Heathrow in the early morning hours of a gloriously sunny day—not your average English weather. We decided to spend one night in London to break up the long journey and give our bodies the needed pre-trek rest. Upon arrival at the hotel, we went straight to bed and had a three-hour nap. In the afternoon, after a long walk in Hyde Park and London's West End, we stopped at a local bookshop and purchased a copy of Ernest Hemingway's *The Snows of Kilimanjaro*. Then we headed to the National Gallery for a brief visit. Afterward, we had a short rest by the fountain at Leicester Square before meeting up with publishing friends for a relaxing dinner at an Italian restaurant on the quiet Jermyn Street, a side street off of busy Piccadilly Circus that's known for men's shirt shops (very expensive ones that the Brits love but Italians would not want to be seen dead in). The next day, after a leisurely breakfast, a nice stroll around Mayfair, and an early afternoon snooze on the grass at Green Park, we picked up our bags from the hotel and took the Tube back to Heathrow Airport to catch our 7:15 PM flight to Nairobi, Kenya.

On board our nine-hour flight to Nairobi, I read Hemingway's short stories, watched BBC News, browsed through the in-flight magazine and tried—unsuccessfully—to get some sleep. I say "unsuccessfully" because I was seated next to a young, animated Kenyan passenger who kept talking nonstop—to me and everyone else around him—for the entire flight. Not only that, he used the flight attendant call button, which he discovered right after take off, as if it were a video game. During the meal service, when the flight attendant asked him for his choice of chicken or beef, he opted for chicken. After removing the foil wrapper, he tapped the flight attendant on her shoulder, a gesture she did not like at all, and complained bitterly about the white rectangular piece of "rubber" resting on a bed of white rice. "Miss, miss," he shrieked, "I asked for chicken; this is not chicken!" Looking annoyed, she answered, "It is chicken, sir." "It is not," he fired back, "where is the leg, where are the wings, the neck—I don't see any." Angrily, the flight attendant took back the chicken and plunked a beef container on his tray. Satisfied with himself, he winked at me and smiled, and went on to eat the whole thing down to the last grain of rice.

Our Kenyan friend—we'd now known each other for several hours and he had already invited us to visit him and his family in Nairobi—calmed down after the chicken incident (and the malfunctioning headphones incident, and the bag not fitting under the seat incident) and let me have a little rest before our descent into Nairobi International Airport. The plane touched down at around 6:00 AM local time and we rushed to the gate to catch our connecting flight to Kilimanjaro. Unlike in Boston or London, going through security at the gate was a breeze—no taking off shoes, belts, watches, and the like. Even the security attendant, whose job was to monitor the handbags on the computer screen as they were scanned, was absent when our backpacks came off the belt on the other side. (He was on a bathroom break, we found out later.) What was most amusing, though, was my incident with the water bottle, which I carried through security when I wasn't supposed to. After being told off—albeit in a friendly manner—the security guard smiled and said to me, "Okay, this time, enjoy it." I thought to myself: "Wow! This would never happen at an airport in Europe or the US."

Unfortunately, the friendly folks at Precision Air, the carrier we were flying with to Kilimanjaro, were not very precise with their departure schedule. We sat in the departures lounge for over three hours before a ground attendant announced, by bringing her cupped hands to her mouth and yelling, that we would be boarding shortly. Fifteen minutes later, as we walked over the tarmac toward the plane, a small 30-seater with propellers, I couldn't help but notice that one of the airplane tires was too low and may have needed some air. "Do you think this plane has a flat tire?" I said to Hildi as we approached the steps at the rear end of the plane. Feeling a little alarmed, I walked over to the landing gear, squeezed the tire with my thumb, and gave it a kick to make sure it was not flat. Other passengers confirmed my suspicion by nodding in agreement.

As it turned out, all my fears were unfounded. The 50-minute flight from Nairobi to Kilimanjaro International Airport was very pleasant and the landing was as smooth as could be. While we flew, high above the clouds at an altitude of 15,000 feet, I wondered what it would feel like to stand with my arms spread wide on top of a mountain even higher than this airplane's cruising altitude. I felt my heart drop the instant I heard the captain announce that we could now see Mount Kilimanjaro from the window on the left side of plane. Immediately, all the faces on the airplane turned in the direction of the mountain. And, wow! There it was, majestically holding its snow-capped head high above the clouds! It was the most spectacular view I've ever seen—our very first encounter with the natural wonder we would spend the next eight days getting acquainted with. I was totally mesmerized. And I continued to stare at the mountain until it disappeared from view.

—

On the ground, as we disembarked from the plane, I could feel the mild East African breeze caressing my sleepy face. "Karibu!" we heard the soft voice of the ground attendant say as she directed us to the terminal building, "Welcome to Tanzania." Inside, we hurried through passport control, picked up our duffel bags, exchanged some money, and headed outside, where we were greeted by a wild array of colorful East African birds hovering about the terminal entrance. Competing for our attention were two dozen or so smartly dressed taxi drivers, all wearing light

Mount Kilimanjaro as seen from the airplane

blue shirts, black suits, and long pointy shoes. We immediately spotted our tour operator's representative, who had a minivan waiting to drive us to our hotel in nearby Moshi.

The town of Moshi, the capital of the Kilimanjaro Region, is situated in the north of Tanzania, close to the Kenyan border, a mere 205 miles south of the equator. With an altitude of approximately 2,920 feet (890 meters) above sea level, Moshi sits at the base of Mount Kilimanjaro. Together with the city of Arusha to its west—known for the Arusha National Park, at the base of the 14,764-foot (4,500-meter) Mount Meru, on the eastern edge of the eastern branch of the Great Rift Valley—it is one of the country's most-visited tourist destinations and a major contributor to its economy. Given their proximity to the Serengeti National Park, the famous Ngorongoro Crater and Conservation Area, Lake Manyara, Tarangire National Park and other attractions, Moshi and Arusha serve as starting points for visitors on safari or hiking trips.

Arusha National Park with Mount Meru in the background

The drive to Springlands Hotel, a popular hangout for mountaineers and safari-goers, was quite an eye-opening experience. We'd both been to Africa before, but this landscape had a distinct feel and smell to it. From the moment we left the airport, the beauty and charm of the land and its people began to unfold in front of our eyes. We passed massive fields of corn and sunflowers—on both sides of the road and as far as the eye could see—carpeting the landscape in green and yellow, two of the four colors of the Tanzanian flag. The sight of long-legged Maasai tribesmen tending their flocks of goats and sheep—in their traditional red blankets and holding wooden *irinkan* clubs and gourd containers—was a delightful surprise. I've always been fascinated by the proud Maasai warriors, whose ageless customs and rituals have survived against all odds. For centuries these nomads dominated much of eastern Africa and were renowned for their strength, courage, and resilience. They clung stubbornly to their traditions as they defied colonialism and Western influence for nearly 70 years. On the way, our driver entertained us by telling us a funny story about the Maasai footwear, which is made out of used car tires and has the exact same rounded shape in the front as in the back. "That's why their enemies were confused all the time and could never tell which way the Maasai warriors were going—you see, all because of the shape of their shoes," he chuckled. Nevertheless, it was sad to witness how the Maasai's nomadic way of life is quickly being eroded by newly imposed government reforms, restrictive land rights, and pressures to modernize.

Along the highway, as well as on the dusty and bumpy dirt roads leading to Moshi, I was struck by how graceful the women looked in their colorful African attire, which was in stark contrast to their brown dwellings made of sun-baked mud and cattle dung. Some women walked with buckets or sacks balanced on their heads and with babies strapped to their backs; others fussed about their neatly arranged fruits and vegetables at roadside stands; and others sat behind sewing machines on the sidewalk with customers lined up for their while-you-wait dresses or alterations. Men on bicycles were everywhere. It was quite amazing to see how ingenious they were in transforming bicycles into shops.

Yes, bicycle shops with multilayered displays of socks and underwear, with children's toys and live chickens, or with firewood stacked ten feet high. Seeing them maneuver these shops-on-wheels around pumpkin-size potholes in the roads was like watching a highly skilled circus act. On the final turn onto the dirt road that led to our hotel, next to Moshi Brewery, we were followed by a band of very young neighborhood children who waved to us energetically and yelled *jambo, jambo*, which means "hello" in Swahili—the boys with big brown eyes and wicked smiles and the girls with short cropped hair and shy looks. They retreated as we approached the large metal gate of the hotel.

—

Inside the compound of Springlands—an unpretentious, well-run hotel in full view of Mount Kilimanjaro—we were greeted at the reception counter by a hostess with a tray of a refreshing orange drink. With the key to our room, we were handed a note from Jetta that welcomed us and reminded us that we had a 5:00 PM briefing with our expedition guide. This gave us about three hours to get some sleep, shower, and get ready. I had barely closed my eyes when I heard a knock on our room door. It was Jetta. She came to greet us and tell us about her chance encounter over breakfast with Guri, a major in the Norwegian air force, who asked if she could join our group. Guri was a UN Observer based in Juba in Sudan. She was approaching the end of her tour of duty when she decided to climb Mount Kilimanjaro before heading back home to Norway. Hildi and I had no objection to having a younger, fit, air force major join us as an expedition partner. Guri would have gone on a solo climb had she not met Jetta earlier that day.

At the briefing, which of course didn't take place at 5:00 PM as planned, Bruce, our guide—who swaggered and looked as relaxed as could be when he arrived an hour late— spread a large map of the mountain on the table and showed us the Lemosho route we'd be taking the following morning. He pinpointed our campsites at the different altitudes, answered all our questions, and

made sure that we all had the necessary gear for the trek. When asked about the weather, he told us that he expected good conditions during our hike. We were all relieved to hear this, especially after we'd heard about the blizzard on the summit two nights before when he and a group of 24 hikers had to endure knee-deep snow conditions on the glacier.

At age 28, Bruce is one of the most sought-after guides to Kilimanjaro. He is highly experienced, well-trained, and speaks good English. Having climbed Kili well over 100 times as guide, he knows every inch of the mountain like the back of his hand. He also knows everyone in Moshi and could assemble the best qualified supporting crew—assistant guides, cook, porters—for the trek. I could tell from the onset that we were in good hands and that we were going to get on well with him. So before he left, I asked jokingly: "What kind of an African name is Bruce?" We all laughed when he explained that he was named Bruce by his mother who got hooked on watching Bruce Lee flicks when she was pregnant with him. On this note, we ended our meeting and agreed on an 8:00 AM departure. I knew right away that this meant 9:00 AM at the earliest—we're in Africa now and everything is *pole pole*. (*Pole pole* means "slowly" in Swahili; it was our guide's most frequently used climbing command on the mountain.)

At least half a dozen languages and accents could be heard as we walked into the outdoors dining hall of our hotel. The place was packed with people of all ages and from all parts of the world: Americans, Brits, Danes, Swedes, Dutch, Germans, French, Spaniards, and others. Some were there with their families to go on safari; others came alone to discover inner clarity and peace; but most had one goal in mind: to set foot on the roof of Africa, the summit of Mount Kilimanjaro. Most—except Basil, our chatty Tanzanian waiter, who had grown up in the shadow of the mountain but never had the desire to climb it. Basil was a fixture at the hotel, and his unforgettable smile greeted us breakfast, lunch, and dinner. He knew all the patrons by name and we were impressed that he remembered ours even after our week's absence on the mountain.

Amid much excitement and talk of the following day's adventure, we left the dining area and retired to our room after wishing good luck to all the climbing folks we'd met at our

communal table that evening. In the garden, on the way to our room, we waved goodbye to Basil and stopped for a minute to look up at the bright, starlit night sky. It was two days after full moon, yet the East African moon was in *pole pole* mode and in no hurry to leave. Before going to bed, I gazed one last time into the distance at the imposing view of the ice-capped natural sculpture called Mount Kilimanjaro, an image that stayed with me through the night and until the early morning, when a wake-up knock on our door sent us rushing to get ready for departure.

THE MOUNTAIN AND THE PEOPLE

Only those who will risk going too far can possibly find out how far they can go.
—T. S. Eliot

Mount Kilimanjaro is the African continent's highest mountain and, therefore, one of the seven summits. It rises nearly 16,000 feet (4,875 meters) above the East African plains and lies 3 degrees south of the equator (213 statute miles at 03° 05' S latitude, 37° 23' E longitude), on the northern border of Tanzania, close to southeast Kenya. It is the tallest mountain in the world that can be climbed without technical equipment. You don't need ice axes, crampons, or ropes to reach its highest point, the Uhuru Peak, at 19,340 feet (5,895 meters)—only a willingness to endure fatigue and strenuous conditions for several days, especially the steep, icy, seven- to eight-hour rough ascent from the last camp to the summit.

A geological wonder that towers above the Great Rift Valley, Kilimanjaro is a mountain formed, sculpted, and molded by the natural forces of volcanic fire and glacial ice. It was born about three-quarters of a million years ago when molten lava coming from three main centers broke through the cracked surface of the earth and shot upward, revealing volcanoes and forming cones and craters. It is now a massive volcano—technically three volcanoes—with two peaks Kibo (19,340 feet/5,895 meters) and Mawenzi (16,893 feet/5,149 meters), since Shira, the oldest, has long collapsed. Mawenzi, the second highest and the most difficult to climb, lies about seven miles east of Kibo, and is separated from it by a beautiful dusty desert called the Saddle. It, too, suffered major erosion that left it with a jagged peak that requires rock-climbing skills to reach. Kibo is the youngest and has the highest summit on its steep, snow-covered rim: the Uhuru Peak. It has three concentric craters and is considered dormant rather than extinct. Its last eruptions occurred some 350,000 years ago, but to this day the surface of its inner Reusch Crater (0.8 miles/1.3 kilometers in diameter) remains too hot for ice formation and is known to vent sulfurous gasses from fumaroles in the Ash Pit (600 feet/180 meters deep) nestled in its center. The ever-changing millennial patterns of Kibo's spectacular glaciers and the effect of the intense equatorial sun, which heats up the lava rock underneath and melts the ice from the bottom rather than the surface of the glaciers, continue to gradually alter the shape of the mountain.

Mawenzi (16,893 feet/5,149 meters),
the second-highest peak on Kilimanjaro

Sadly, there are no historical documents that record the ancient or pre-colonial history of the mountain and its inhabitants. The only known references from antiquity are one mention in the second century CE by Ptolemy, the Alexandrian astronomer and geographer, another attributed to Chinese traders who saw "a great mountain west of Zanzibar" some seven centuries ago, and one by a thirteenth-century Arab geographer by the name of Abul Fida. There is also no agreement among historians and etymologists on the origin of the name Kilimanjaro, which bears no resemblance to any word in Chagga, Maasai, or Swahili, the language most widely spoken today in Tanzania. While one can find some similarities to words in all three languages when the name Kilimanjaro is divided into two parts (*Kilima* and *njaro*), the absence of exact matches renders these findings inconclusive. But the names of the two main peaks Kibo and Mawenzi are without a doubt Chagga in origin and come from the terms *kipoo* (meaning snow) and *kimawenzi* (meaning broken top).

From recent history, we know that the land around the base of the mountain, with its fertile volcanic soil, is home to the Wachagga people, commonly known as the Chagga. Artifacts, pottery fragments, and stone bowls found on the lower slopes of the mountain tell us that the Chagga, a Bantu people, set up their farming communities some 200 or 300 years ago, and, with abundant water from its forests, cultivated the land ever since. They lived in clusters of thatched beehive huts and drank *pombe*, a homemade beer made by fermenting bananas and millet in a hollowed tree trunk. The Chagga—one of the largest, wealthiest, and most educated ethnic communities in Tanzania today—were originally made up of many different clans and tribes (Keni, Machame, Kibosho, Marangu, Moshi, Arush), which raided one another's villages and took slaves as battle spoils. It was only in the latter part of the nineteenth century, when faced with colonial rule, that they became unified. During these times, they set up successful coffee-growing cooperatives that brought them an improved standard of living and better schooling. Today they continue to strive for advancement and higher education, with confidence and pride, and a strong identity defined by unity and respect for their ancestors.

Lava rock formations

But having been on the receiving end of some intense work by European missionaries, the Chagga soon abandoned most of their traditional beliefs and practices in favor of Christianity and Western culture. Some adopted Islam, but most became followers of the Roman Catholic or Lutheran church. Marealle, the crafty and shrewd chief of the Marangu tribe, a non-believer himself, outsmarted the Europeans and played it safe by having one son baptized as Catholic and another as Lutheran. To Marealle, this probably was no different from the tribal practice of marrying a daughter to an enemy chief in order to make peace or benefit from an alliance.

Driving around Moshi and the surrounding areas, one cannot help but notice the abundance of nicely built concrete churches that stand out among the mud brick and corrugated tin-roofed dwellings in poor neighborhoods. An incident we experienced on a walk in downtown Moshi was also telling of how relentlessly hard Christian churches work at multiplying their flock. We had stopped for a minute close to a mosque when a chubby Christian nun in gray ran up to us and said in English: "Don't walk or stand around here. It is not safe—bad people." I couldn't understand it at first; the place was buzzing with people and everyone we talked to on the street seemed super friendly. We were intrigued to see how many people entering the mosque left their shoes with the shoe shine/shoe repair man stationed on the adjacent sidewalk—he was doing brisk business that day. We were also amused to see an unattended spice merchant's cart, whose owner, we were told, had gone to the mosque to pray. "If the spice merchant feels safe about leaving his shop unattended, and loads of others feel safe about leaving their shoes on the sidewalk, why then should we feel unsafe?" I wondered. Back at the hotel, I mentioned this incident to the receptionist who assured us that it is quite safe to walk around anywhere in downtown Moshi.

Downtown Moshi: street corner shoe shine and repair stand, and a spice merchant's stand

The Pioneers

Because it's there.
—George Mallory, when asked why he wanted to climb Everest

It is quite astonishing that Kilimanjaro, whose massive white dome can be seen from miles and miles away, remained unknown to anyone in the Western world until its discovery in the middle of the nineteenth century by Johannes Rebmann, a German missionary stationed at Rabai Mpya near Mombasa. Rebmann's first glimpse of the snows of Kilimanjaro took place in 1848, on the Kenyan side of the mountain, east of the border town of Taveta, which is now part of the Tsavo West National Park, a wildlife reserve from which the view of the mountain looks particularly spectacular. His claim was initially shunned by leading European geographers of the time, who refused to believe the existence of snow so close to the equator, until it was later confirmed in 1861 by Baron Karl Claus von der Decken who reported encountering a blizzard upon reaching an altitude of about 14,000 feet (about 4,270 meters) before returning home to tell about it.

Baron von der Decken's expedition was hailed as a success by the Royal Geographic Society and he was awarded a gold medal, the society's highest honor. This opened the door to several important explorations in the last two decades of the nineteenth century. European adventurers lured to the mountain reached higher and higher altitudes each time, but exhaustion and cold conditions prevented early climbers from reaching Kibo's peak. On his first attempt, Dr. Hans Ludwig Meyer, a German geographer, came as close as 1,300 feet from the top before he was forced to turn back after conditions on the mountain worsened and fields of ice stopped him from going any further. Unfazed by the danger, Dr. Meyer returned to the mountain two years later, this time better equipped to tackle its icy conditions. He brought with him Ludwig Purtscheller, an accomplished alpine guide, Chagga guide Yohana Lauwo, five porters, and all the technical equipment available at the time. He—together with Purtscheller—finally conquered the highest point on the edge of Kibo's crater rim on October 6, 1889, becoming the first white men to successfully reach the summit. Upon reaching the peak, Meyer erected a German flag and named it Kaiser Wilhelm Spitze—it was, after all, German East Africa. Climbers today are reminded of this momentous day by the two memorial plaques at Marangu Gate, one dedicated to Hans Meyer while the other commemorates "the first guides and porters who assisted the first climbers to reach the summit of Mount Kilimanjaro."

On the heels of their success on Kibo, Meyer and Purtscheller turned their attention to climbing Mawenzi, which proved far more challenging. Here they faced major obstacles and had to give up after their third attempt. Nevertheless, Meyer's failed attempt earned him the honor of bestowing his name on Mawenzi's summit, which is now known as Hans Meyer Peak. His pioneering ascents were important for those who came after him, such as Oehler and Klute, who reached Mawenzi's summit in 1912, and Sheila MacDonald, who in 1927 became the first female mountaineer to reach its peak.

By this time, the Marangu trail (now part of the Marangu Route, known to tourists as the "the Coca Cola route" because Coke cans are available for purchase at the huts) had become well established and a few huts, built at different altitudes, became rest stops and sleeping quarters for adventurers heading to Kibo. The inner Reusch Crater was named after the Reverend Dr. Richard Reusch, who went on to summit Kilimanjaro numerous times and in 1926 was the first climber to spot the frozen leopard Hemingway wrote about in *The Snows of Kilimanjaro*. In 1978, Reinhold Messner, who climbed Everest in that same year, pioneered the Western Breach Route—an extremely dangerous, steep wall—and reached the Uhuru Peak with his colleague Konrad Renzler. This route is now closed to climbers by the Kilimanjaro National Park Authority (KINAPA) after rocks and boulders tumbled down and claimed the lives of three American climbers on January 4, 2006. Today the Uhuru Peak—renamed after Tanzania's independence in 1961, meaning "Freedom Peak" in Swahili—is reached by thousands of climbers each year who flock to the mountain to follow in the footsteps of the early pioneers and experience the breathtaking scenery, from the roof of Africa, of the legendary snows of Kilimanjaro.

Following page: The Western Breach

The Trek

In wildness is the preservation of the world.
—Henry David Thoreau

On Kilimanjaro, nature trumps all. The brashness, exoticism, and the variety of climate zones of the approximately 60-mile/97-kilometer climb to the top are unmatched anywhere else in the world. The six-day climb starts from the cultivated lower slopes with dry blistering heat, through a lush, wet rainforest jungle, into heath and moorland zones, all the way up to the desolate alpine desert landscape and the steep, exposed arctic summit area, where virtually no plant or animal life can survive. It is a trek that pushes you to your limits, as your body battles exhaustion, under sometimes unpredictably harsh weather conditions—heat, rain, fog, wind, snow—on a variety of challenging terrains: muddy, dusty, rocky, snowy, and icy. But the adventurous are amply rewarded with an unforgettable experience, in many more ways than words can describe.

Our departure started the way things often do in that part of the world: slowly—*pole pole*. After a hurried breakfast, we waited—and waited—by the front gate until our guide, assistant guide, and cook finally arrived in the Land Rover that would take us to the Londorossi Gate, the entrance to Kilimanjaro National Park. Our duffel bags were hurriedly loaded onto the roof rack of our Land Rover, and we were soon on our way, after making only one quick stop in downtown Moshi to buy water—enough to last us for the rest of the day. The drive to the gate was a harrowing two-hour journey along a narrow, twisty, and bumpy one-lane dirt road, which led to the foot of the mountain on the western side. At one point, we hit a monster bump in the road and I found myself flying off my seat and hitting my head against the roof. "Damn it! That's all I needed," I thought as I landed on the edge of my seat, "an injury before we've even started climbing." For the rest of the trip, I held on tightly with both hands to the metal pole next to me and braced myself every time I anticipated a bump in the road.

Upon arrival at the Londorossi Gate (7,380 feet/2,250 meters), we were greeted by a passing rain shower, which sent us straight back to the car for shelter, after first registering with the park rangers. While we ate our boxed lunches, the porters unloaded, weighed, and reloaded our duffel bags onto the roof rack of our 4WD, and our guide disappeared to pay

the park entrance fee and take care of all the necessary paperwork. We then drove for about an hour through a forest track lined with Mexican pine (*Pinus patula*) and cypress (*Cupressus lusitanica*) trees until we reached the Lemosho Glades (6,890 feet/2,385 meters) trailhead. On this tighter road with muddy, crater-size potholes, our 4WD stalled three times, each time taking our driver about ten minutes under the hood to get the car restarted. But the driver, who would pop his head out from under the hood every now and then to give us a reassuring smile, always seemed calm and confident that the 4WD would restart. When the vehicle moved again we held our breath and glued ourselves to our seats. It was pretty scary to watch how the 4WD slid left and right on the mud and came within a hair's distance from villagers walking on the side of the road with potato sacks balanced on their heads. We were all relieved when we finally made it to trailhead in one piece and laughed when the driver—a small, cheerful guy with mischievous eyes—presented us with his tattered comment book and asked each of us to write something in it.

It was early afternoon by the time we arrived at the Lemosho trailhead, the starting point of our climb. Our porters were already waiting for us with the tents, cooking equipment, and food baskets spread on the ground. We introduced ourselves to the entire team and I chatted with some and tried to learn their names. Unlike the guides, the porters spoke very little or no English, and we spoke no Swahili. Since they were going to be our constant companions on the mountain for the next eight days, I made an effort to try to remember their faces. Before we hit the trail, I tried to make conversation with Faustin, the cook, who spoke some English, so I asked him about the contents of one of the baskets on the ground. He told me that it contained sixty fresh eggs. "Wow, sixty eggs! Why so many?" I asked. "Ten eggs for each client," he answered. Granted I was never very good at math, but I could easily calculate that ten eggs per client for four clients did not add up to sixty. I went back to him and said: "You know, Faustin, ten plus ten plus ten plus ten add up to forty—not sixty!" He looked up at me, rolled his eyes, and answered me as an elementary school teacher would answer a student: "No, sixty, because twenty get broken on the way. Then you are left with forty—ten eggs for each client." That simple!

We started our walk along a forest trail with our guide Bruce in the lead. It was warm, misty, and damp. The trees—African Pencil Cedar (*Juniperus procera*), Podo Evergreens (*Podocarpus milanjianus*), East African Camphorwood (*Ocotea usambarensis*)—were dripping with rainwater, turning the forest floor into a slippery mud rink. Despite these conditions, the porters zoomed by with 40-pound sacks balanced on their heads and were already out of sight. At that moment, it felt as though we had the forest all to ourselves. I slowed my pace and let everyone walk ahead and then stopped. Now I could listen to the otherworldly sounds of the rainforest without the distraction of shuffling boots. I closed my eyes and listened to the different sounds and textures coming together. What I heard was an ensemble of an incredible variety of sounds—a natural rather than an artificial beauty—conducted by the slow up-and-down movement of tree branches in the wind. Against a drone accompaniment provided by the mild whisper of the wind I could hear the vibrato of a nearby spring and the faint ruffling melody of the tree leaves. A rhythmic element introduced by falling berries and drips of rainwater sounded like an African talking drum in the distance. Every now and then the rhythm would be punctuated by the occasional loud but gruff *khaws* of the Hartlaub's turaco (*Tauraco hartaubi*)—a dark-crowned bird with violet-blue wings and tail and a very dark red bill, endemic to East Africa—or the *wa-wa* and *aaah-aaah* of the large Silvery-cheeked hornbill (*Bycanistes brevis*), with the gigantic bill and the dull cream casque. As I resumed my climb and listened to the noisy and exuberant calls of the turacos, I became convinced that hip-hop must be the birds' genre of choice; definitely not the quiet, meditative, mood-setting sounds preferred by their forest companions.

While Mount Kilimanjaro is a hydro-geographical wonder, it is the forest, by virtue of its ecosystem and species diversity, that is the jewel in the crown. Nearly 96 percent of the water flowing from the mountain originates in this forest belt, the lifeline that provides drinking water to the villages below and irrigation for the banana, coffee, and other plantations on the

The beginning of the Lemosho trail

lower slopes. Such ideal conditions, in a forest that receives rain almost year round, create a multitude of habitats for numerous varieties of living things, including 140 or so species of mammals. Two species of monkeys inhabit the rainforest: colobus and blue monkeys. They are both fairly large and have thick fur. We encountered a family of blue monkeys (grayish blue in color) on the move, but it was the sight of the colobus that made my day and left me with a lasting impression. Up close we saw a commanding performance by three beautiful colobus—black and white with long bushy snow-white tails—gracefully leaping like circus trapeze artists from branch to branch in tall trees.

Soon our trek began to take on a dreamlike quality, as though we'd passed through a gate into a fairyland. The trees and the hundreds of plant species endemic to Kilimanjaro are the main attraction of this semi-tropical rainforest, which stretches from about 6,000 to 9,200 feet (1,800 to 2,800 meters) on the lower slopes of the mountain. Bearded lichens (*Usnea barbata*) dangle from tall trees like shredded mosquito nets, mosses hug tree trunks and branches and paint the forest with vibrant greens, and giant ferns dance in fragmented sunlight. The deeper we ventured into the heart of the forest, the more the forest revealed its inner beauty.

We stopped several times to admire and photograph the great variety of wildflowers, especially the elegant violets (*Impatiens pseudoviola*) and the dazzling red-and-yellow impatiens (*Impatiens kilimanjari*) endemic to the mountain. On the trail our guide was constantly identifying flowers and plants like a botany professor. He talked about different animal species as if they were old friends and advised us on what to look out for and what we were likely to see in the forest. Giraffe can sometimes be seen in the forest, but large animals such as antelopes, bushbucks, duikers, and leopard tend to be shy and quiet and stay well hidden in the bushes. During a short break, after walking for nearly two hours, Bruce wrote in my journal the Latin name of the Hartlaub's turaco we had seen earlier and said, "You know I got an 'A' grade in the flora and fauna course I took as part of my training." Sounding impressed, I asked more bird questions, but he explained that we were unlikely to see any this late in the afternoon. "The best time to spot birds in the forest would be at dawn," he said.

Right: wildflowers of Kilimanjaro; following pages: giant ferns and bearded lichen

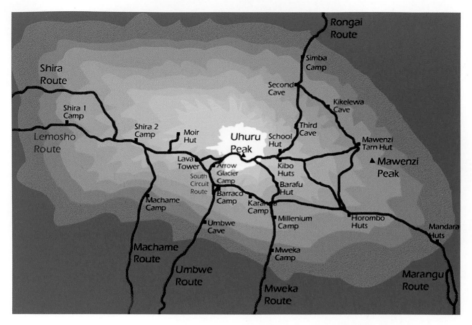

Bird species that inhabit the forest include ibis, olive thrush, brown woodland warbler, white-starred bush robin, a variety of parrots and pigeons, and many others.

Through thick vegetation and with intermittent drizzle we walked for another two hours or so before we reached our first campsite at Big Tree Camp (9,120 feet/2,780 meters); also known as Forest Camp or *Mti Mkubwa* in Swahili. My shirt was damp and marked by white salt lines under my arms. But the climb so far had been moderate and the terrain mostly good. We passed only a couple of steep places where we had to hold on to tree branches for balance, and one area where the mud was ankle deep. On arrival at the campsite, we found the porters waiting for us with tea and popcorn. They had already set up camp and erected our tents. From the smell of food I could tell that Faustin had been busy preparing dinner. I wondered how many eggs had survived the first part of the trek.

Darkness was sudden and swift, as though someone had turned down the dimmer switch, and the temperature dropped rapidly. After a short rest in our tent we heard a soft, deep voice calling "Halloooooo, halloooooo!" It was Adam—a soft-spoken porter with huge, sad, soulful eyes—announcing that dinner was being served in the orange dining tent. Adam wore a woolen hat that covered his ears and forehead—rapper-style—and had a very calm demeanor. He had a multi-part job: he woke us up in the morning and brought us tea; he boiled drinking water for us; and he served us our meals. I got used to hearing his voice on the mountain and it stayed with me long after we returned home. Hearing his sweet "Halloooooo" waking us up every morning brought smiles to our faces and made it easier to get out of our cozy sleeping bags in time for our departure. I became very fond of Adam, whose ambition was to improve his English so one day he could be promoted to assistant guide.

I could smell the steaming potato soup as we entered the orange dining tent. All four of us were famished after this afternoon's trek, so hardly any words were exchanged for the first fifteen minutes. This changed, though, after we'd each had two helpings of soup. We had moved on to the pasta and to getting to know each other a little better. Throughout dinner I kept thinking of how amazing it was that this mountain had brought us together—such a diverse group of people from different parts of the world and with different backgrounds. I could not have done a better job selecting our climbing group. There was Jetta from Scotland who wrote walking and climbing guides; Hildi, a photographer born in East Germany who worked in academia and specialized in East German films; Guri, a major in the Norwegian air force on break from her tour of duty as a UN Observer in Juba, Sudan; and I, a US-based publisher born in Beirut, Lebanon of Palestinian parents. Our little orange dining tent felt like a mini international summit of sorts; we discussed everything from wars and occupations to globalization and global warming. Soon Bruce, our Tanzanian guide, came in and joined us, to ensure that Africa was also represented, and to brief us about the next day's trek.

We chatted with Bruce for about twenty minutes, asked questions about the next day's climb, and then we all retired to our tents. I spent the rest of the evening with the sounds of the forest serenading me to sleep.

At 7:30 the next morning I found myself near the bottom of our two-person tent when I heard Adam's voice calling "Halloooooo!" The ground on which the tent was erected was muddy and sloping downward. "If we'd had a heavy downpour during the night, our tent would have ended up back where we started at the Londorossi Gate," I jokingly commented during breakfast. But despite this, I woke up feeling rather refreshed and energetic and ready for the day's seven-hour climb. At around 8:30 AM, after a hearty breakfast of hot porridge, we each packed about three liters of drinking water (which Adam had boiled the night before) into our backpacks, and we hit the trail—an eight-mile trek to Shira 1 Camp (11,480 feet/3,500 meters), an elevation gain of 2,360 feet (720 meters).

Under sunny skies, our climb continued through the forest for about an hour or so. Along the way, we were shadowed by a massive eagle that gave an impressive aerial display as it tumbled and soared above us as we walked. Our guide identified it as an African Crowned Eagle (*Stephanoaetus coronatus*), a broad-winged and long-tailed eagle with a rough crest. We observed the gradual change in forest density with increasing altitude and the trees became smaller and smaller the higher up we climbed. As we departed the top of the forest, the trail got steeper and we entered the giant heather zone at approximately 9,200 feet (2,800 meters). Here two hardy giant heaths dominated the landscape: the Philippia (*Philippia excelsa*) and the Erica trees (*Erica arborea*), nearly twenty feet (six meters) tall and eerily draped with lichen. An array of wildflowers scattered among the trees added splashes of bright color to an otherwise drab landscape. Red-hot pokers (*Kniphofia thomsonii*) were quite abundant on the trail and so were the spiky white-and-pink helichrysums (*Helichrysum meyeri-johannis*) and the exotic-shaped sugarbush flowers (*Protea kiliman-jarica*), with their upright and stringy white petals, which we stopped to photograph on several occasions. Since I don't consider identifying flora as one of my strengths, I got really excited when, a few feet from the trail, a flower I could identify caught my eye. It was a splendid—albeit lonely—light red gladiolus (*Gladiolus watsonioides*) hiding behind some thistle and sheltering from the wind and the other unpredictable elements nature might unleash at this altitude.

Sugarbush (left), Gladiolus (right)

Most of the precipitation in the heath and moorland zones (9,200–15,000 feet/2,800–4,500 meters) comes from the mist, which arrives in late morning and stays until late afternoon, and from the occasional heavy downpour, which turns the stark landscape into an overnight floral display. But while the mist brings in enough moisture that some plants can survive at this high altitude, animals find it difficult to live and are rarely seen on the increasingly barren higher slopes. One creature, however, that feels quite at home at this altitude is the four-striped grass mouse (*Rhabdomys pumilio*)—but so do the raptors that hunt it for food.

Birds that venture up to the higher slopes are active just before dusk. They include the small, dark brown alpine chat (*Cercomela sordida*), which has a partly white tail, the attractive marsh owl (*Asio capensis*)—with dark brown back and wings—common in the moorland zone below 10,000 feet (approximately 3,000 meters), and raptors that can be seen hovering about in both the moorland zone and the higher alpine desert area at 15,000 feet (approximately 4600m). On Kilimanjaro, raptors that can be spotted indulging in flight displays as they look for prey include the augur buzzard (*Buteo augur*), a large black-and-white buzzard with a distinctive red tail, and the mountain buzzard (*Buteo oreophilus*), a small, dark-brown-and-white buzzard. But the bird that never seems to want to leave you alone—in any zone, and at any altitude—is the large, noisy, scavenging, tent-visiting, expert backpack-opening, white-necked or white-naped raven (*Corvus albicollis*). This bird has absolutely no mountain manners whatsoever. One morning, a large raven stopped within two feet of our open tent door. For a few minutes he (or she—I couldn't tell) just stood there staring at us without moving. I threw my shoe out in an attempt to get rid of him. In the end, he flew away, but only after nibbling at my shoe outside the tent.

Cooler, dryer air set in as we climbed further up the increasingly arid trail. The mountain was nearly deserted. Unlike other popular routes, the Lemosho route is blessedly free from the daily pounding of hikers' feet and allows one to encounter true solitude.

Erica trees in the heath and moorland zones

There is nothing like a hit of solitude to help you sort out what's in your head and figure out what's important in life. Again I stayed behind and let everyone go ahead in order to walk alone, "to trample those appetites that spring from earthly impulses," as eloquently put in the fourteenth century by Francesco Petrarch, the first man to climb a mountain in search of psychological redemption (Mont Ventoux is the South of France). Here again I experienced the emotional potency of being alone on the mountain, of getting back in touch with nature, of being in a place where nothing manmade could be seen or heard. I stopped moving for a moment and could instantly hear the music of the mountain at this altitude. A lone bird—probably an augur buzzard—floated gracefully overhead. But contrary to the orchestral and percussive sounds I'd heard earlier on the lower slopes, on this spot nature performed a more subdued musical arrangement, an earthy composition played by what felt like a string quartet dominated by the mellow, soothing, and hypnotic sounds of the cello. I sensed that on this vast, remote, and wild terrain, the musicians have room to move, to stretch out and to really listen to each other as they improvise and transform mute barrenness into musical beauty.

Further ahead, the trail crossed the Shira Ridge at approximately 11,800 feet/3,600 meters and then dropped gently to the day's final destination, the Shira 1 Camp (11,483 feet/3,500 meters), situated nearby a stream on the picturesque Shira Plateau. It was around 3:00 in the afternoon when we arrived at the campsite, a little ahead of schedule. Upon our arrival, Adam brought us steaming hot tea and popcorn as well as a bowl of warm water for washing. With the tent door open, I lay my head on my duffel bag while my eyes drifted in the distance. We were in the middle of nowhere. Yet I felt happy. I had enjoyed the climb so far and I liked the peaceful surroundings of our campsite—especially the ability to restore my connection to the wilderness. Being on this remote spot of the mountain gave me a true appreciation for its wonder and beauty and fired my desire to climb further and see more. I was also touched by the warmth and smiles of our porters, guides, and climbing partners. Above all, I cherished the intimacy that was forming between us all as we became one another's only source of stimulation—something that would be hard to replicate elsewhere.

Shira 1 Camp

Adam's call to let us know that dinner was ready was eagerly awaited since we were all very hungry and it was getting cold. Within barely a minute from the sound of his "Halloooooo!" we were all sitting inside the orange dining tent warming our bellies and savoring every bit of delight from the sumptuously hot carrot soup—a specialty of Faustin, our gourmet mountain chef. The soup was followed by pasta and then pineapple and finger-long bananas for dessert. By that time, my headache, which had begun in the late afternoon, had intensified. When I mentioned it during the course of the evening, I immediately detected concerned looks on the faces of my colleagues. While everyone was sympathetic and reassured me that it was a natural reaction to altitude gain, my announcement caused a shift in our conversation and triggered a lengthy discussion of altitude sickness. Interestingly, though, we all avoided the one question that was on everyone's mind: What would happen in the event that one of us was unable to continue with the climb? Toward the end of the evening, Jetta, our straight-talking Scottish friend, was the one who brought it up. It didn't take long, though, for us all to agree that in such an eventuality the rest would continue on.

We all went back to our tents after a short briefing with Bruce, during which he shared with us the next day's plan and we informed him of our collective decision should one member of the group be forced to turn back. I heard Adam's voice outside the tent as I drank the last of my water with two extra-strength headache pills. "What good timing!" I said as I unzipped the tent door and handed Adam our empty water bottles and camelbacks for refilling with boiled water. The air I felt on my face was crisp and frost was beginning to form on the outside of the tent. Happily, I slipped into my warm sleeping bag and rested my achy head on a bag containing two soft rolls of biodegradable toilet paper—to have something comfortable underneath my head but, more importantly, to avoid having to search for them in the dark in case nature called in the middle of the night.

—

Shira Plateau. Following pages: Lichen varieties

"Headache's gone!" were the first words I uttered when I woke up in the morning—and what a good feeling that was! It was such a relief. I woke up in a spritely mood; I even preempted Adam's morning greeting as soon as I heard the shuffling of his feet approaching the tent. This time, it was I who said "Halloooooo, halloooooo!" when I unzipped the tent door to receive the thermos of hot tea he brought us. It was nearly eight o'clock in the morning and all of a sudden I felt a strong craving for fried eggs. Strange, I thought, since I hardly ever eat eggs when I am at sea level. Hildi and I quickly packed our duffel bags and headed to the orange dining tent to meet Jetta and Guri for a breakfast of porridge and scrambled eggs. Luckily, there were still some unbroken fresh eggs left to satisfy my craving and give me the needed energy boost for the day's climb.

We started the third day's trek around 9:00 AM with a gentle walk across the Shira Plateau—one of the mountain's most beautiful attractions—on moorland meadows. It was another glorious day—clear, warm, and intensely sunny. While the walk up the Plateau seemed fairly mild, we were constantly reminded by our guide to climb slowly—*pole pole*—to avoid altitude sickness and give our bodies time for acclimatization. Three hours into our steadily upward walk, Bruce pointed to the right at two Kilimanjaro landmarks: the Shira Needle and the Shira Cathedral, two dramatic peaks on the southern ridge of the Shira Plateau. He also told us to keep an eye out for eland, gray duikers, red duikers, jackals, and buffalo, but we did not see any that day. What we did see, though, was a magnificent view of the entire Western Breach, the dangerous, icy climbing route to Kibo's peak that was closed by the park authorities.

To avoid encountering any possible climbing groups that may be camped at the popular Shira 2 Camp (12,795 feet/3,900 meters), our guide opted for Moir Camp (13,697 feet/4,175 meters), the least visited camp higher up on the mountain, for the third night's stay. Off the main trail, we took a left artery and walked up for another hour or so before stopping for lunch at Fischer Camp (12,894 feet/3,930 meters), named after the late Scott Fischer, the renowned American mountaineer who arguably pioneered the Lemosho route. Here, we were all pleasantly surprised to see Adam waiting for us with tea and biscuits, and Faustin crouching against a boulder preparing lunch. It was such an unexpected treat to have a good cook with us on the mountain. Faustin, I found out during a later conversation, had attended a prestigious culinary training college and apprenticed at the Njuweni Hotel near Tanzania's capital, Dar es-Salam, before deciding to return home to Moshi.

After lunch we all had a ten-minute lazy lie down on the ground, which made it difficult to get up and resume the climb for an additional two-and-a-half hours to Moir Camp. But climb we did. And we arrived at the camp just in time to enjoy the fantastic views overlooking the Shira Plateau before the veil of darkness covered the sky and the cold temperature kept us confined to our tents.

My head started pounding around the same time as it had the previous night. This time, though, it was throbbing and was coupled with nausea and stomach discomfort. I knew right then and there that I had become the first casualty of altitude sickness and that made me very upset. In the past few days the smell of Faustin's cooking had sent hunger signals from my stomach to my brain; this time, though, it caused my nausea to intensify and sent me straight on a tent rampage looking for a plastic bag. Luckily, Hildi came to my rescue in the knick of time and produced a Ziploc bag in which I violently emptied the contents of my stomach. I felt some relief and I tried to get some rest. I desperately needed to get my mind off what had just happened, but returning to the book I was reading was not the smartest idea. Reading about Elizabeth Gilbert's eating, praying and loving across Italy, India, and Indonesia caused what felt like volcanic tremors in my stomach and almost induced another eruption.

Naturally, I skipped dinner that evening and this caused some concern among my colleagues and doubts about my ability to continue with the climb. Upon hearing about my state, Bruce came by the tent to check on me. From the wrinkles on his forehead and the movement of his eyebrows I could tell he too was worried. Sounding very serious and professional—like a doctor in an examination room—he asked me a slew of questions in order to evaluate my condition. He took a minute to think and then he advised me to drink lots of water and urged me to start taking the altitude sickness pills my travel doctor had given me for such an eventuality. Reluctantly, I took one. I rested my head on my duffel bag and closed my eyes. Half an hour or so later, my headache and nausea disappeared—completely. "Like magic!" I told Hildi when she returned to the tent after dinner.

Still worried about whether I'd be forced to turn back if my dizziness and nausea returned, I spent most of the night wide awake—with a plastic bag in hand.

—

Moir Camp. Following pages: View of Kibo (left); view of Shira Plateau (right)

"No eat, no summit!" was Adam's reaction to my reluctance to have anything other than tea for breakfast after my nausea of the night before. True, I felt very hungry and a little weak, but I didn't want to take any chances and have to stay behind or descend if my condition worsened. Adam, though, wouldn't take no for an answer. He just stood there—motionless—outside our tent staring at me with his brooding eyes until I finally got out and walked with him to the orange tent to have breakfast. Inside the tent, I took one look at Jetta, Guri, and Hildi and I could immediately tell what was going through their minds. It felt as if I had walked into a funeral home. Without saying a word, and to everyone's astonishment, I proceeded to eat like never before. It was the first time I'd had this big a breakfast. Even Adam looked surprised when he brought us some tea and saw me eating. When I caught his eye I winked at him, gave him the thumbs up, and said: "Now we summit!"

Having replenished my energy and restored my spirit, I was soon back to my old self and ready to face any challenges the day's climb might bring. Thankfully, by the morning of the fourth day, my body had acclimatized well and it was the last time I suffered any effects of altitude sickness on the mountain.

Our fourth day trek started at 8:30 AM with Costa, our assistant guide, in the lead, followed by the four of us, then Fortunatus, our second assistant guide, at the very end of the line. Costa, I could instantly tell, was very conscientious and genuinely attentive. He took his job very seriously and was well acquainted with the mountain. He was trained by his brother Bruce, and like Bruce he had introduced many urban climbers to the lore of Kilimanjaro, knowing every trail, every campsite, every stream, every rock formation, every buzzard. Costa (short for Constantin) was a towering figure, which disguised his quiet and shy personality. He was studying at a local college to become a chartered accountant and only worked on Kilimanjaro during the summer and on school breaks. At first, it was a bit of a challenge to get Costa to talk. I asked all the questions and he gave brief and polite replies. It was only when I asked him to teach me Swahili did he become more relaxed and talkative. "You really want to learn Swahili?" he asked, with a chuckle that crunched his tanned cheeks.

Following pages: On the way to Lava Tower

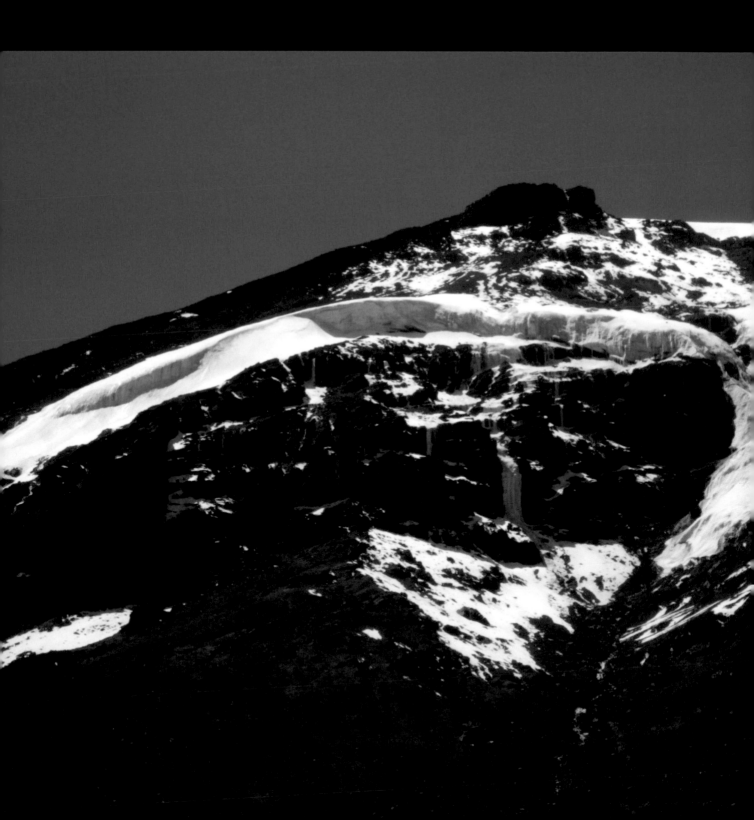

"Yes, we have another four days on the mountain—that's plenty of time for me to learn if you'd be willing to teach me some words and sentences," I answered. I explained that it would be nice for me if I could communicate with the porters in their own language—even a little. The porters did not speak any English and I wanted to be able to greet them as I passed them on the trail, to be able to thank them when they filled our water bottles, to tell them how much we appreciated the work they did, and say good morning and good night. He graciously agreed and said, "Okay, you ask me what you want to say and I will tell you how to say it in Swahili." Over the course of the next few days, I made a list of English words and sentences in my notebook and whenever I saw Costa on the trail I went up to him and asked him to give me their Swahili equivalents.

It didn't take long for me to put what I had learned from Costa into practice. At the sight of the first approaching porter, I prepared myself by looking up a few words and sentences in my notebook and repeating them to myself over and over again. When Musa—a tall, muscular porter in black sweats and a yellow tank top—was about to bypass me, I turned around and greeted him with the familiar "*jambo*" (hello!). After he returned the greeting, I surprised him by asking "*Habari yako?*" (How are you?), to which he answered "*Nzuri sana*" (fine, thank you) and then slowed down his pace so we could chat some more. Other porters I passed on the trail were equally surprised when I asked them questions in Swahili or used Swahili words they did not expect to hear from a climber. Soon words like *kwa heri* (goodbye), *twende sasa* (let's go now), *nimechoka* (tired), *pole pole* (slowly), *asante sana* (thank you very much), *lala salama* (good night), and many others became familiar sounds to my ears and easier for me to pronounce. This was especially true in the case of words that were similar to Arabic, my mother tongue, or came from the same Arabic root word.

Coming into close contact with our Tanzanian porters and guides, the one thing I could not help noticing was the range of footwear they wore. From flip flops to sandals to sneakers with missing laces and boots with fist-size holes, the "shoes of Kilimanjaro" rank among the most amazing sights encountered on the mountain. One porter on our team had shoes that

looked like those donned by circus clowns—at least five sizes too big. Another wore "air-conditioned" tennis shoes with multiple rips in the front and on the sides. Yet regardless of how bad the porters' footwear looked, one could never tell from the way they danced up steep hills, raced down muddy slopes, or maneuvered around hair-raising cliffs with heavy loads balanced on their heads. I had to laugh thinking back about Hildi's and my preparations for the journey, how we agonized over whether our canvas hiking boots would be sufficient or whether we needed to bring heavy-duty leather mountaineering boots. Watching our porters, whose sweat flows down every trail on every route, sprint in their flimsy, worn-out footwear was a humbling reminder of the poverty and hardships endured by people in the region. Their dismal shoe situation stayed on my mind and bothered me the entire time we were on the mountain until the evening before our departure, when several guides and porters joined us for a farewell drink—all wearing trendy, well-ironed clothes and, to my total amazement, snazzy-looking boots.

I, for one, was glad that I had comfortable hiking shoes for that day's steep trek on the increasingly rocky landscape from Moir Camp to Lava Tower (15,190 feet/4,630 meters), the looming 320-foot (98-meter) high volcanic mass that is often climbed by those with rock-climbing skills and energy to spare. As we hiked east up the mountain for over four hours, our trail twisted and turned before we ascended the rocky scree path to the imposing Lava Tower, where we stopped for our lunch break. Looking up at the free-standing volcanic remnant, one is dwarfed by the immense size of this weathered Kilimanjaro landmark. In its shade, we had a half-hour rest from what had been the most demanding and toughest climb so far. This gave me a chance to catch my breath, write some observations in my notebook, and review the Swahili sentences I'd learned from Costa earlier in the day.

At 15,000 feet (4,600 meters), the air got dryer and colder, and the landscape was transformed yet again. By the afternoon, the intensity of the equatorial morning sun had diminished and everyone could feel the drop in pressure. With less oxygen in the atmosphere, we got increasingly breathless; our hearts and lungs had to work much harder to oxygenate

Lava Tower

our bodies. Repeatedly, our guides warned us to remain hydrated and go slowly. Wary of the effects of altitude sickness, they recited the mountain's mantra—*pole pole*—more frequently than before. "Today, we climb high and sleep low to help you acclimatize," our guide explained before we resumed our walk down to Barranco Camp (12,960 feet/3,950 meters) located in the beautiful Barranco Valley below the Western Breach and the Great Barranco Wall.

The two-and-a-half-hour walk to the campsite was fairly steep and a tad rough on the knees, but the drop in altitude made it easier to breathe. As we descended to the valley below, patches of short grasses, Erica bushes, and Philippia shrubs dotted the semi-desert landscape. We were stopped in our tracks by the amazing sight of the giant groundsels (senecios and lobelias) ahead of us. These distinctive and unusual-looking plants-on-steroids looked like props straight out of a Hollywood dinosaur movie set. The tree groundsel (*Senecio Kilimanjari*), with its green crown of leaves and yellow flowers, was particularly impressive. This monster plant can grow to a height of up to twenty feet (about six meters), helped by its dead leaves, which do not fall off but instead wrap themselves around the plant and act as insulation and protection against frost. The smaller endemic species, the *Lobelia deckenii*, the mountain's other main floral attraction, was equally striking. It has hidden blue flowers and can grow to about ten feet (about three meters) in height. It is a favorite of the most beautiful and colorful bird on the mountain, the scarlet-tufted malachite sunbird (*Nectarinia johnstoni)*, which I spotted on our walk down the Barranco Valley. It is a big, dark-green sunbird with scarlet pectoral tufts and long tail feathers. For about a minute it hovered above a lobelia plant and attempted with its long curved beak to get to the flies that lived at the plant's base. Sadly, the sunbird flew away before I was able to call Hildi to photograph it.

Giant tree groundsels. Following page: Lobelias.
Pages 92–93: Barranco Camp (left); view of Kibo (right).

We were all pretty exhausted by the time we arrived at the campsite, but the spectacular surroundings made me want to explore despite my achy feet. Without going far, though, we had superb views of both the Barranco Wall behind us and the Western Breach in front. At one point, I stood right below the Western Breach and looked up at the majestic White Mountain and the remnants of the ice caps that covered it. I had goose bumps. Totally engrossed and in awe, I thought to myself: "Words can describe Kilimanjaro and photographs can speak of its beauty, but nothing comes close to expressing the unique thrill I am experiencing at this very moment." The Kibo peak looked so close, so reachable, and yet we were more than two days away from our summit bid.

Suddenly, the light changed. It was just before sunset. For a brief moment, the mountain and the sky above turned into a warm blue-and-orange pastel painting with a few brushstrokes of white. Behind me, with camera in hand, Hildi clicked away as the golden sunset flared, capturing a truly special moment, an image that graces the front cover of this book.

—

Over breakfast the next morning, we found out that Jetta had suffered a mild form of altitude sickness the previous afternoon. She told us that it hit her in the exact same spot on an earlier climb eight years back. At the time, she had been researching the Machame route for the climbing guide she was writing. Jetta looked pale and a bit under the weather, but we all knew that this was not about to stop her from going ahead. Fortunately for us all—but especially for Jetta— day five was meant to be an acclimatization day, with limited elevation gain and lots of rest, to enhance our chances of success.

The short trek to the next campsite was only 4.5 miles (about 7 kilometers) and took no more than four hours. We started by going up a steep ridge to the Great Barranco Wall, which required quite a bit of scrambling on rocks, climbing the wall to a point where the icefalls of Kibo's southern glaciers soared overhead, and then descending to Karanga Valley, where we camped for the night.

Climbing the Barranco Wall

On the way, we passed many giant rock formations, dramatic volcanic sculptures, which have over the years acquired names. One massive boulder in particular, which Fortunatus, our assistant guide, pointed out to us was the funny-looking, turtle-shaped rock formation named Kobe.

We arrived at Karanga Camp (13,240 feet/4,035 meters) in the early afternoon, which meant that we had the rest of the day free to relax or explore. I opted for the former, but first, before I could do anything else, I desperately needed to take care of one very important thing: wash my hair and get cleaned up. I jokingly commented that it would be disrespectful to the mountain gods to show up at the summit in such a dreadfully disreputable state. After five days on the mountain my body had started mass-producing strange odors; my hair had begun to form dreadlocks and had the smell of dirty socks. It was my last opportunity to do something about it, since Karanga Camp, situated nearby a stream, was the final water point on the route.

Much to the amusement of my colleagues and the bewildered stares of our porters, I used the small bowl of water that Adam brought us for our hands on my head—half to shampoo, and half to rinse. I then went into the tent, undressed, and with Hildi's help proceeded to scrub every inch of my body with biodegradable wet wipes, removing layer after layer of sweat and dirt. Oh, what a nice feeling that was! With renewed vitality and high spirits, I felt like going out for a jog in the fresh mountain air. Instead, though, I decided to save my energy for the summit attempt, so I sat on a rock outside our tent and let my hair dry in the sun and my lungs take in all the air they could handle.

I spent the rest of the day reading and napping, napping and reading. Hildi walked around and took photographs; Guri, the fittest among us, went on a hike and explored further afield; and Jetta wrote in her notebook and drilled Bruce for information for her climbing guide. Resting in the tent, I thought about the kids—Leyla in New York, Hannah in England, and Maha in Palestine—and what they might be doing at that particular moment. I recalled when I first told the girls of our plans to climb Kilimanjaro and how they thought we were crazy. "Dad, you're over fifty," they said. How I wished that they could have come with us and shared the countless unanticipated pleasures we'd encountered, each more special and more surprising than it was possible to imagine!

As we watched the sunset disappear behind the jagged peaks of Mawenzi, we felt the temperature drop rapidly, to a bone-chilling level. We were all bundled up with several layers of clothing when we gathered for dinner in the orange dining tent. When Adam brought us tea, we hurried to warm our hands by wrapping them tightly around our steaming hot tea cups, which got colder after each sip. Dinner was followed by a short briefing during which Bruce reminded us again that Karanga would be the last place for water, and the necessity of carrying with us all our water needs for the next 36 hours.

—

In the morning, each of us carried about three liters of water in our backpacks as we set out on the final day's trek before our summit attempt. Jetta's altitude sickness had disappeared; she looked cheerful, and so was everyone else after a good night's rest.

For the first part of the hike, heavy mist made it difficult to see in front of us. We headed east for about two hours, to the point where our route intersected with the Mweka trail, which is normally used as the descent route from the Kibo summit. At the intersection, we made a left turn and then ascended a ridge through a largely bleak and desolate alpine desert landscape in the direction of Barafu Camp (15,225 feet/4,640 meters). On this vast stretch of empty arid terrain hardly any vegetation was visible. The intense morning sun, the frigid, sub-zero temperature at night, the thin air, and the very low precipitation at this altitude made it impossible for plants or animals to survive. Apart from tussock grasses and hardy red and green lichens, which grew on the lava rocks strewn all over the landscape, only some species of the spiky and dry everlasting flowers (*Helichrysum*) could withstand such extreme conditions.

The place looked so deserted, so lifeless, so silent. It resembled a film set of an old spaghetti western after the filming had ended and everyone had left. I could hear, literally, nothing.

Karanga Camp

View of Kibo from Karanga

Karanga Valley

Barafu Huts

I was amazed, though, to find out how looking at the great expanse of space combined with the amplified muteness of the mountain at 15,000 feet sort of relaxes you, allows you to unplug in a remote environment; it melts away basic desires, fills you with serene tranquility far away from life's harsh realities, puts your mind at ease, comforts you. In a sort of strange way, it sets a rhythm, a tone, a different mindset to prepare you for the big summit night ahead.

Upon arrival at Barafu Camp in the early afternoon, we were met with icy-cold gales of wind. It suddenly felt bitterly cold; we all dug out our woolen hats and warm jackets from our backpacks and huddled together for warmth. "This is what it's going to be like from here on," I commented to Guri, who put on a thick, olive green, Norwegian air force–issue sweater underneath her red down jacket. Showing off my recently acquired knowledge of Swahili words, I said: "There is a good reason why they call this camp Barafu; it means ice in Swahili."

Inside one of the round, green Barafu huts, a park ranger sat with a blanket wrapped around his upper body. He looked disheveled, lonely and cold. His dry facial expression seemed to say: "You people are nuts! I have to do this for a living, but why are you here? Why put yourself through this when you could be sitting comfortably on your warm living room couch, watching TV, and drinking beer?" Dull as it was, his job was important, especially in the unlikely event of an emergency. He had to make sure that every passing mountaineer was registered in the book so that the park authorities would have a record of who's attempting a summit climb on any particular day.

The seven- to eight-hour summit trek on this route normally commenced from Barafu Camp at midnight. Several other groups were already there by the time we arrived. I watched some porters battling the wind as they tried to pitch their tents on the exposed campsite. I also recognized some fellow climbers we'd met on the lower slopes, sheltering in a small group behind the ranger's hut. We chatted with a lot of people on that day—climbers from Germany, Denmark, Sweden, the USA, England, and other countries. There was a lot of excitement in the air. We'd all made it this far and the Kibo peak now seemed closer than ever. We exchanged stories, shared snacks and advice, high-fives, and wished each other luck.

While we were mingling and meeting other climbers, our guide had an idea. He asked us if we would be up to climbing further for another hour or so and camping not on Barafu, but on a narrow, stony ridge higher up the mountain. He warned us that the camping conditions would be a little harsher, the wind fiercer, and the air a little thinner. But he said that the advantages outweighed the disadvantages: it would shave an hour off the time it would take us to reach the summit; it would give us an hour's head start and hence avoid the crowds; and we'd be a little less tired and have more energy than if we were to start our summit bid from Barafu. These factors should enhance our chance of reaching the Uhuru Peak, so we agreed with Bruce and he went off to obtain permission from the ranger.

It didn't take long before Bruce returned with a satisfied look on his face. We didn't ask him how he was able to convince the ranger to let us do this. Bruce had his ways. Besides, he knew everyone, he was well liked, and he was highly respected on Kilimanjaro.

The slog up to the rarely used Kosovo Camp (16,200 feet/4,938 meters)—an elevation gain of nearly 1,000 feet (300 meters) from Barafu and about 3,000 feet (900 meters) from the day's starting point at Karanga—was rocky and ghostlike. We hiked up in a northwesterly direction. Loose scree littered the landscape and a deafening symphony of silence filled our ears. Every now and then, the silence would be broken by the sound of our chatter, our heavy breathing, or our guide's voice warning: "*pole pole*," and "be careful, don't twist your ankles on the rocks." A twisted ankle, like acute mountain sickness, would spell the end of your summit climb. So we walked slowly and carefully, watching every step. The steep ascent and the high altitude meant that we needed more frequent breaks. We were above the clouds. As we climbed higher and higher we could feel the pressure dropping and the air getting thinner. We reached nearly 16,000 feet (4,878 meters) in altitude. At that point, my heart was beating noisily. It sounded like a base drum echoing loudly and rhythmically behind a rapper's voice. Except there was no rapper and there was no voice on this remote stage. Without even noticing it at first, I found myself rapping underneath my breath. Against the rhythm of my loud-beating heart, I was repeating the Swahili word *pole pole* after every third heartbeat.

Thump, thump, thump, *pole pole*, thump, thump, thump, *pole, pole*. I couldn't get it out of my head; it went on and on until we finally reached the campsite and I was distracted by Adam's voice greeting us on arrival.

"You don't know how long I've been thinking about this cup of tea," I told Adam as I threw my backpack inside our flapping tent. It was windy and he could barely hear me. With a hot cup of tea in hand, I did my usual walk around to check out the new campsite. Behind me to the east was Mawenzi, partly cloaked with the shadow of Mount Kilimanjaro. With its sunny top and its dark bottom, it looked awesome. It resembled a proud African queen—curly hair, long dress, bare shoulders—showing off her beauty. I turned around and looked up in the opposite direction. There was Kibo, the undisputed king of the mountain. Etched in the mountainside above, I could see the beginning of the well-beaten path we would be traversing to the summit at midnight. It looked shockingly steep. A blow down from the blizzard that had taken place earlier in the week had obliterated part of the trail. With my eyes, I traced its zigzagging path to the point where it intersected the ice field and was no longer visible.

An early dinner call interrupted our short rest. Outside the tent, the wind was cold and strong. During the course of our dinner, our orange dining tent collapsed on us and the porters struggled to keep it standing. But while the wind was blowing outside the tent, inside our faces were glowing with pre-summit excitement and looked pink-red from the steam

Mawenzi cloaked with the shadow of Kibo

Kosovo Camp

of the hot soup Faustin had prepared for our final alpine meal. Having done the summit climb before, Jetta became the target of all our questions that evening. Serious ones like: How cold is it likely to get at the summit? How many layers should we wear? Will our water freeze on the way up? Will the camera work at such high altitude? And not so serious ones like: How does one pee on the glaciers? Is it true that a Viagra pill can help you summit?

Alas, what promised to be an engaging and entertaining discussion of the art of peeing on ice was quickly aborted when Bruce walked in to give us his final briefing. After a quick rundown of the plan for the next 24 hours, Jetta asked if she could start the summit climb one hour before the rest of the group. She expected to be super slow and didn't want the rest of us to be held back and get cold. Bruce agreed to accompany her and said that we would catch up with them on the mountain and then summit together. He concluded the briefing by reminding us to check our equipment before going to sleep and advising us to dress warmly for the summit climb.

We retired to our tent and hurriedly prepared our gear: we put fresh batteries in our headlamps and camera; we dug out all the thermal clothes and fleece jackets we'd brought; and we made sure that our packs had our water, hiking poles, and some snacks. As I slipped into my super warm, -15° F (-26° C) sleeping bag, I reminded Hildi to keep the camera close to her warm body inside the sleeping bag so that it didn't freeze. We had about three hours before our wake-up call. We tried to get some sleep but it was impossible to get even a wink. The sharp flapping noises of the wind beating against our tent and the deep thumping of our ultra-excited hearts sounded like Japanese Taiko drummers testing their instruments before a performance. The loudness, the mixed rhythms, and, of course, our anxiety all conspired to turn us into sleep-deprived high-altitude zombies.

"We ate, we laughed, and we stayed wide awake all night. That's how I shall always remember our summit night," I told Hildi before I fell into a deep sleep literally half an hour before our wake-up call.

THE SUMMIT

There are only two mistakes one can make along the road to truth;
not going all the way, and not starting.
—Buddha

Come back in half-an-hour, Adam," I said as I turned around on my side to go back to sleep. It was 11:30 PM when Adam stood outside our tent and tried to wake us up with his usual "hallooo," to start our final ascent. He was bearing hot tea and biscuits, but that was not enticing enough to drag us out of our warm sleeping bags and into the frigid temperature outside. But knowing that he would get into trouble if he didn't do his job, Adam was persistent and kept saying: "Nooo, time to go to the summit, please wake up."

In inky darkness, Adam waited patiently outside our tent until I unzipped the tent door to receive the tea thermos and he could see that we were actually awake. Cold air blew into our warm tent and gave us unwanted chills. Without exchanging any words, Hildi and I sat up and dressed hastily, putting on every piece of clothing we had in our possession at the time—every jacket, fleece, Polartec, and every pair of thermal underwear. In all, I wore six layers on my upper body and four on my legs, including two pairs of long johns, sweats, and waterproof ski pants. With so many layers on, I looked like a bear who had just feasted on a moose. I struggled to zip up my jacket and I couldn't get out of the tent without a shove.

Under a luminous night sky, we began our grueling trek up the mountain on a steep, python-shaped gravel path that twisted back and forth. It was a little after midnight when we started marching in formation behind Costa, our assistant guide. Our goal was to reach the summit between six and seven in the morning, in time to experience the beautiful Kilimanjaro sunrise. The air was thin and crisp; the wind forcefully alive; and the night hike dauntingly boring. I passed a good part of the first hour talking to Guri about her experiences working with refugees in Sudan. But as interested as I was in the topic of our conversation, I was unable to sustain it. At nearly 17,000 feet (5,200 meters), I began to pant step after step and had little spare energy for talking. My mouth was dry, my lips semi-frozen, and my tongue lacked the will to move.

Higher up the mountain we were lashed by powerful winds as we forged on through heavy scree and ice between the Rebman and Ratzel glaciers. The summit trek did not require the use of ropes, ice axes, or crampons, but it was quite challenging and not for the faint of heart. I found it both physically and mentally taxing. At first, I felt confident of my abilities—not so when I came face to face with the biting wind and the cross currents on the exposed ice field on the way to Stella Point (18,650 feet/5,685 meters) on the crater rim. I slipped on the ice time and time again and was forced to stop in order to catch my breath. Each time, though, our guide urged me to keep moving. In a soft voice, he muttered words of encouragement. "You're doing great, keep moving, *pole pole*," he would say every time I stopped. "We're nearly there," he'd reply every time any one of us asked how much farther we had to go—even when we were hours from reaching the top.

Apart from one short rest when we caught up with Jetta and Bruce on the trail, the bone-chilling temperature prevented us from stopping for any length of time. Sometimes even pausing for a drink required too much effort at high altitude. At one point I felt thirsty and sheltered behind a rock to have a drink of water. Repeatedly, I bit hard on my camelback bladder but nothing came out. It was totally frozen. Even the energy bar I got out of my backpack pocket felt like a block of ice. In the end, Costa let me have a sip of his water, which instantly froze as it splashed my moustache and cracked when I said to him *asante sana* ("thank you" in Swahili).

We moved with utmost caution, one foot in front of the other, hauling ourselves up on what seemed like an endless frozen stairway to heaven. With my head down and my eyes hypnotically fixated on Costa's heels, I pushed myself forward on the slick ice. Thump thump thump *pole pole*, thump thump thump *pole pole*, the song from the day before came back to me. And like the day before, I repeated the word *pole pole* in my head after every third heart beat—over and over and over as we climbed up and up and up through the night. Soon the steady, hypnotic rhythm of my mountain song put me in a sort of a trance, essentially blocking from my mind the effects of the winds raking my face and the jolts of pain felt by my feeble knees.

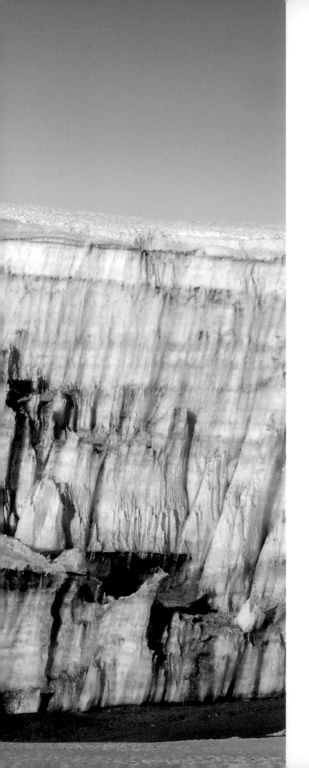

After four hours or so on the path up to Stella Point, I stopped for a moment and looked back to see how Hildi was doing. A minute later Guri arrived. Together we waited for a few more minutes but there was no sign of Hildi or Jetta or our guide Bruce. There was simply no one behind us. Looking down the mountain, all I could see far in the distance were tiny points of light from climbers' headlamps scattered like dazzling jewels on the curved trail below and blending harmoniously with the glittering night skies above. "We lost them," I said, sounding alarmed. "We cannot wait," Costa blurted assertively when I told him that I wanted to wait for Hildi so we could summit together. Realizing that his instantaneous reaction must have sounded a bit harsh, he looked at me and said politely and in a gentle tone: "Let's go, please. It's too cold." He put his hand on my shoulder and urged me on by saying: "We will freeze if we don't keep moving."

As we continued our ascent toward Kibo's peak, the lack of sufficient oxygen, the harsh weather conditions, and debilitating fatigue began to take its toll on our bodies. Beyond 18,000 feet (4,585 meters), I needed to take several breaths for each step forward. When the ice field incline reached a level even steeper than the highest setting on my gym's treadmill, I felt I couldn't go any further; when I saw climbers half

Kibo glaciers

my age turning back due to exhaustion or altitude sickness, I came close to giving up. But each time Costa would boost my confidence by reciting his "We're nearly there!" line. "I've heard that before," I told him after I got fed up hearing him repeat the same thing when we still had hours to go. But that time Costa was right. We were just minutes away from reaching Stella Point on the crater rim.

When we arrived at Stella Point (18,650 feet/5,685 meters), I yelled instinctively, in a voice that echoed up the mountain and was loud enough to be heard by the summit gods: *nimechoka* ("I'm tired" in Swahili). I even surprised myself; in the state I was in, I didn't think I could remember any of the Swahili words I'd learned earlier. As I leaned my achy body against a large boulder to rest for a few minutes, I kept hoping that the next climber passing through would be Hildi. My body was warm underneath all the layers I had on, but my hands were not. As we stood still amid a wind tunnel, I could barely feel my fingers from the cold. Worried about hypothermia and frostbite, I asked Guri to dig out two packets of hand warmers from my backpack pocket. She handed them to me and I shook them rapidly, took the wrapping off, and stuck them inside my gloves. Warmth made its way to the palm of my hands fairly quickly, but since I was wearing gloves instead of mittens the warmers could

View of Mawenzi from the Uhuru Peak

117

not reach my fingers, which remained icy and without feeling until the sun came out and we descended to the lower slopes.

One look at Guri before we resumed our climb was enough to tell me that she was not well. She had suffered from altitude sickness on our final approach to Stella Point but told no one about it. When she felt dizzy and nauseous, she stopped, rested a little, and drank lots of water. Judging that her symptoms were not severe enough to warrant an immediate descent, she decided to continue on. We were only 45 minutes to an hour away from the Uhuru Peak and turning back would have been a huge disappointment for her. For the rest of the climb, Fortunatus, the assistant guide she was climbing with, kept a close eye on her and carefully monitored her symptoms to make sure that they did not get worse.

Powered by my strong desire to see the spectacular views from the top and my eagerness to witness a Kilimanjaro sunrise, my legs kept moving forward and my arms pushed harder on my poles. I was breathing faster and deeper. Fortunately, though, the final stretch to Uhuru was comparatively easier and less strenuous than what we had already gone through in the past five hours. For the remaining hour or so, we walked mostly on soft snow and scree up a gentle incline that led to the top of Kibo, an elevation gain of 689 feet (210 meters) from Stella Point.

Sunrise on the summit of Kibo

Gasping for air, I arrived at the summit at around 6:15 AM, feeling as though I had just breathed my last breath. "Congratulations! You are now at Uhuru Peak, Tanzania, 5,895 meters, Africa's Highest Point" read the wooden sign. It also indicated that at this height, we were at the summit of the world's highest free-standing mountain—meaning not part of a range—and the world's largest volcano. Costa, who was at my side the entire summit climb, gave me a congratulatory hug. Jokingly, I said to him "No more 'we're nearly there,' Costa," as I barely managed to crack a smile from the side of my frozen lips. There were no tears of joy, no leaps in the air, but I was clearly over the moon. It was a uniquely thrilling moment—albeit a sad one since Hildi wasn't there to share it with me.

"I can't believe we're actually here," I told Guri as she arrived with Fortunatus minutes later. I was so pleased to see them. I was worried about Guri's altitude sickness and was concerned that it may have intensified on the final climb. We all hugged and managed to take a couple of photographs of each other in front of the summit sign before the batteries in Guri's digital camera started acting up from the extreme cold. Together, we waited, shivering, for darkness to make its final exit and the warm sun to come up on the horizon.

On the summit, an overpowering sense of solitude prevailed. A lifeless silence calmed even the most restless of souls. We were alone. I was totally immersed in my thoughts—am I really on the roof of Africa?—when the sound of the wind broke the stillness and a group of cheering young climbers arrived speaking a language I did not recognize. They all stood behind their unfurled football club banner while their guide took their photograph. Soon after, three older climbers from Germany, all wearing high-tech mountaineering outfits and black gaiters, limped up and posed for a photograph in front of the Uhuru sign. Watching other climbers come and go, I thought of Hildi, Jetta, and Bruce. I kept hoping that they would show up any minute so we could celebrate our achievement together. Sadly, they were nowhere to be seen.

We stood there watching the powerful sun inch up and bring with it a cornucopia of bright colors blending together and transforming the landscape before our very eyes. I have never seen a peak so glorious in the morning sun as Uhuru. And nothing compares to the breathtaking views you get from the top of Kibo. Stretching in all directions, as far as the eye could see, its changing vista of color was stunningly beautiful; the silvery glaciers we'd been unable to see in the dark were an astonishing sight. You could not look down at them without feeling certain awe. To the west we had a clear view of Mount Meru and in the east a white cloud covered the jagged peak of Mawenzi like a stylish hat protecting its head from the equatorial sun.

"Time to descend," urged Costa after he saw me shivering and noticed that icicles were beginning to form on my moustache, not to mention the disgusting frozen snot dangling from my nose, which I was embarrassed to see later on in the summit photos. Despite the sun coming out, the temperature was still well below freezing—around -10° F (-23° C) and that's without taking into consideration the wind-chill factor. We wanted to stay longer and take in more of the amazing scenery, but it was bitterly cold and we needed to move our bodies to stay warm. So after about twenty minutes on the summit, and having lost all hope of reconnecting with our climbing partners, we decided to descend.

Heading down the mountain, I marveled at its unique features, especially those magnificent views we'd missed during our all-night climb: the shining white glaciers, the exquisite natural ice sculptures, the indomitable Mawenzi. I wished I had the camera with me, but Hildi is the photographer in the family and since we were climbing together it made perfect sense for her to be the one carrying the camera. Without one, I resorted to snapping mental photographs with my eyes and ears—all drenched in the sounds of mountain—and saving them in my memory. In daylight, the mountain revealed so much more of its secret beauty.

As I trudged down the mountain, lovely hues of orange and yellow painted the blue-gray equatorial sky. By that point I was beyond exhausted and hoped that my knees would be able to withstand the long journey back. Looking in the distance and seeing other climbers trying to make their way up toward the summit, I was thankful that I was on my way down and not one of them. As I got closer to Stella Point, I was surprised and overjoyed to see that Hildi was one of those climbers I spotted from afar. She mentioned that Jetta and Bruce were not far behind. But before even giving me a chance to digest this joyous encounter, she said in her East German English accent that sounded so much more German than English in thin air: "You have to come wiz me."

"I've summited already," I replied as I tried to explain to her that I was half dead and that my legs would not carry me back up to Uhuru. "No, you have to come wiz me," she insisted. She did not spare a single arctic moment to remind me that climbing Kilimanjaro was my idea and that we promised each other that we would summit "togezer." In the end, I felt I had little choice but to say: "Okay, wiz you I come!"

Hildi and I reached the Uhuru Peak at around 7:30 AM, followed by Jetta and Bruce five minutes or so later. Not in my wildest dreams could I have ever imagined reaching the summit of Africa's highest mountain twice—in the same day.

The Uhuru Peak, Africa's highest point

THE DESCENT

The deepest feeling always shows itself in silence.
—Marianne Moore

After they first appeared nearly 12,000 years ago, the legendary snows of Kilimanjaro are, sadly, and rapidly, turning into the barren slopes of Kilimanjaro. The ice is disappearing at an alarming rate. Estimated to be around twelve square kilometers at the beginning of the twentieth century, Kibo's ice cap is now only two square kilometers. This is due to vastly reduced precipitation on the summit as well as the increase in temperature and the effect of global warming. At this rate of retreat, scientists reckon that the ice cap will be gone by the year 2025.

While glacial melting is one of the most visible signs of climate change and the warming of our planet, the melting of Kibo's ice is not a direct result of the sun's radiation; the pure white, mirror-like glaciers reflect the bulk of the solar heat. It is the absorption of the heat by the black lava rock underneath the glaciers that is largely responsible for the melting, disintegration, and eventual breaking of the ice. Glacial sculpting, on the other hand, is the exclusive master work of the equatorial sun, whose vertical rays, aided by the wind, chisel at the ice day in and day out and create gleaming structures—spiky towers, artful pillars, impressive blue-white ice cliffs—that enthrall you with their beauty.

—

Despite my exhaustion, when Hildi and I stood below the Uhuru Peak sign, I experienced overwhelming joy and satisfaction to be sharing this unbelievable moment, especially after losing each other on the mountain during our night climb. Here we were, on Africa's highest point, a perfect jewel surrounded by beauty in every direction. At that moment, I realized that there's a lot of truth in the popular saying: "The world can't weigh you down when you're standing on top of it." I don't know why the sight of Kibo glaciers with their striking metallic sheen elated me. The pure white wilderness looked particularly stunning in the morning sun, while the arctic silence and isolation reminded me that we were a world apart from our daily existence, in a place where nature's rule is supreme. It was very disheartening to think that one day Kibo might be free of snow and ice, that such glacial beauty may soon vanish.

Aware of the glaciers' precious short life and fragility, I wanted the memory to last. So I walked around in different directions enjoying the views until I could no longer bear the effects of the cold wind on my hands and face. Some hardy climbers with extra energy often descend from the summit to the Ruesch Crater to see the dramatic ice pinnacles of the Eastern Ice Fields; others—like us—admire them from afar. We had a very long descent ahead of us and we felt it unwise to hang about the summit much longer. Having missed a night's sleep, we were very tired; the oxygen level at this high altitude was around fifty percent of what one would normally get at sea level. We were also worried about Jetta, whose speech had suddenly become muddled in the thin air. I couldn't decipher any of the words that came out of her mouth at the summit. But it also could have been my hearing that was distorted; I wasn't sure. Whichever it was, one thing became clear: it was time to descend—and descend fast.

It was nearly 8:00 AM when we started on our way down from Uhuru. Our destination was Mweka Camp (10,105 feet/3,080 meters), situated in the giant heather zone on the upper edge of the forest, a steep, eight- to nine-hour trek down the mountain and a drop in altitude of 9,235 feet (2,815 meters). As I walked into the wind, a few lone teardrops descended from my left eye along a wrinkled trail on the side of my face and down my frozen moustache before landing on my lips. The moisture reminded me how thirsty I was. The last sip of water I'd had was from Costa's bottle hours ago, but I would have to wait for another two hours or so until my water defrosted further down the mountain.

We first retraced our steps back to Stella Point by following a faint track of trampled snow. From there, we took the very steep Mweka Route down, which commenced with a slippery path across the ice field and then followed a rocky trail through the ghostlike alpine desert landscape, where dusty dry earth was the flavor of the day. The Mweka Route is the main descent route for all climbers on five of the six official climbing routes, all except those who ascended via the Marangu Route. It is the fastest, most direct way down the mountain,

Kibo glaciers

which means that it has the steepest incline, forcing you to keep your brakes on for a good chunk of way. We also had to watch out for the piles of rock that erupted from the earth thousands of years ago and were now scattered as though creating an obstacle course all over the desolate landscape.

It is a well-known fact that most mountaineering accidents happen on the descent. So to avoid falling or tripping on loose scree, we descended with caution and used our poles to slow ourselves down and ease the pressure on our knees. A nine-hour descent right after an eight-hour all-night climb was by far the longest and most strenuous bit of hiking I've ever done. We had a brief rest at Barafu Camp, but in some ways that made it harder for us to get back on our aching feet again. It was especially difficult for Hildi, who had suffered a minor knee injury when she stumbled and pulled a muscle on the hike up. On the sharp Mweka Route, gravity forces you to descend much faster than you desire, which made it exceedingly more painful for Hildi than the slow climb of the past six days. While an ointment Guri gave her from her Norwegian air force first-aid kit helped the swelling a little, for the rest of the way down,

View of Mawenzi on the descent

Costa, Bruce, Fortunatus, and I—with Costa doing the most—took turns holding Hildi's arm to ease the pressure on the injured leg.

When Costa was on break from helping Hildi, he walked alone. I grabbed this opportunity to brush up on my Swahili. I went up to him and asked him to give me Swahili equivalents to more English words. He looked a bit weary, but he still managed to crack a smile at my request. To show our gratitude to the porters who spoke little or no English, I wanted to say a few words of thanks in Swahili at the farewell ceremony normally held at the end of the expedition. I thought this would be a nice gesture that would not only show our respect and admiration for their culture, but also express our appreciation for their hard work on the journey. On Kilimanjaro expeditions, the guides and porters perform important and difficult tasks that go largely unnoticed or at the very least underappreciated. They really deserve most of the credit for making it possible for thousands of hikers each year to have a uniquely wonderful experience on the mountain.

Later that morning, we walked under sunny skies, which really lifted everyone's mood. As the temperature rose and I got more oxygen into my lungs, my juices started flowing and my energy soared—energy I didn't think I had. I took off one layer of clothing almost every 2,000 feet (about 600 meters) and I no longer looked like an overgrown bear; instead I was prancing down the slope like a gazelle. And I started to hear music again—not the slow, uphill *pole pole* song I'd hummed in a weary voice while I was nearly breathless on the climb towards Kibo's peak, but a more lively and upbeat version that started with a groovy 2/4 rhythm on the *djembe*. I had to seize the moment. I collapsed my hiking poles and hung them on the side of my backpack, leaving my hands free to drum the 2/4 beat on my stomach and thighs. At first, I played a solid rhythm for several measures to get a feel for the beat and settle on the right tempo. Then, with my hands tapping a different part of my body each time, I went about exploring a variety of percussive sounds. I added a hit here, an embellishment there, until I was finally satisfied with the introductory percussion part of what was to become my impromptu Kilimanjaro composition.

During the hours that followed, the sky changed and changed, every shade of blue, silver, gray. Buzzards glided along, sometimes sweeping down really low as if to listen to my new Kilimanjaro song, which was beginning to take shape. Inspired by the wonderful variety of sounds I heard on the mountain—the birds and the trees in the rainforest, the silent notes in the alpine desert, the raucous wind on the summit, the thumping of hikers' boots on the trail, the sloshing of water in my camelback, my heartbeat in thin air—I soon came upon a catchy melody that stuck in my head. Over and over and over again, I whistled the melody against the drum part I played on my thighs until it all came together and became part of me. All it lacked at that point were some vocals. So when I put my head together to compose the lyrics to the song, I did the obvious thing: I used every Swahili word I'd learned from Costa on the hike. I had so much fun toying with the lyrics, the melody, and the rhythm I even forgot how tired I was and how much farther we had to walk.

I was not yet ready to share my song with anyone and kept it a secret. When I walked alone, I sang it loudly—I should tell you that I have a pretty awful voice—but when my colleagues or our guides were close by I hummed it underneath my breath so no one could hear me. I did this for the entire rest of the way down until we finally reached the Mweka Camp, just as the curtain of darkness began to close, and I collapsed from exhaustion inside our tent.

"Hallooo, congratulations, dinner is ready!" said a familiar voice outside our tent. Of course, it was Adam. We hadn't seen Adam or heard his sweet voice since he'd woken us up for our summit bid at midnight the night before. As I sat up in the tent to greet him, I felt every muscle in my body ache as never before. That evening I could not even muster the energy needed to get out of the tent and over to the orange dining tent less than twenty feet away, where a special traditional Tanzanian meal was being served. Instead, I remained in the tent and munched on leftover trail mix and energy bars. Disappointed that I didn't show up for our last evening meal on the mountain, Bruce came by to see me. As I unzipped the tent door, I saw that he was holding something shiny in the dark. It was just what I needed that evening: two cans of beer.

Later my colleagues told me that I'd missed an amazing meal that evening. Faustin, they said, outdid himself and cooked a really tasty Chagga dish, which he called *Banana Ndiʒi*—his own variation of the traditional East African recipe *Ndiʒi na Nyama* (Swahili for plantains and meat). The traditional curry recipe normally called for beef with onions, tomatoes, and coconut milk cooked with plantains. But on the last night of our seven-night expedition, Faustin had to improvise and use up whatever leftover ingredients he had on hand. So the result was a vegetarian version cooked with bananas instead of plantains, together with carrots, potatoes, and green beans. We later asked Faustin for the recipe, and the traditional recipe is shown here. You can try it as is, cook Faustin's Kilimanjaro *Banana Ndiʒi* version, or experiment by adding your own preferred selection of vegetables.

Ndiʒi na Nyama (Plantains with Meat)

INGREDIENTS
1 cup/250ml water
2 lb/1 kg beef, cut into ½-inch (1 cm) cubes
1 tsp salt
½ tsp black pepper
½ tsp curry powder
½ tsp red pepper
3 tbsp cooking oil
1–2 onions, sliced
2 medium tomatoes, chopped
1 tbsp tomato paste
1 cup/250ml coconut milk (or 3 tbsp butter)
1 bay leaf
3–6 plantains, peeled and sliced

METHOD
• Boil the water in a large pot then add the beef, salt, pepper, and curry powder.

• In a separate pan, fry the onions in the oil until golden; add the tomatoes and tomato paste and cook for a few minutes; then add the coconut milk and bay leaf and let simmer for 5 minutes.

• Add the plantains to the meat and cook until the meat is done and the plantains are tender.

• Combine the onion mixture with the meat and cook for a few more minutes.

• Serve with rice

THE FAREWELL

After silence, that which comes nearest to expressing the inexpressible is music.
—Aldous Huxley

I slept soundly on our last night on Kilimanjaro. Our tent was pitched on a muddy surface that sloped downward, but that didn't bother me the slightest. I slept through the night until dawn, when the squawks and trills of a multitude of birds supplied my wake-up call. Still feeling a bit stiff, I sat up, unzipped a crack in our tent door, and peeked outside; the light still a milky blue, the air thick with new scents, and everything felt damp and sticky from an overnight downpour.

We were camped at the edge of the forest where the land was less arid. Several other groups were camped at Mweka, each with a cluster of tents of a different color. Dotted among the thick bushes with yellow flowers and tall heather that surrounded the campsite, the bright-colored tents—blue, yellow, green, orange—made the place look like a vibrant van Gogh painting with a few black ink blots here and there for the dark, immobile ravens resting on tree branches.

I was not ready to get up yet and breakfast was still an hour away. So I lay quietly on my back and reflected on the intimate experience of the past week. Our wilderness escape was drawing to a close. Eight memorable days had come and gone since we started our trek and it was now time to say farewell to the mountain and the people who had touched us deeply and made this unforgettable journey possible. How could I really express our gratitude to the guides and porters with my limited vocabulary of Swahili? What could I possibly say at the farewell gathering that would leave a lasting impression? Many questions and thoughts circulated in my brain early that morning. We had planned on giving each member of the crew a generous tip to reward them for their exceptional work. And we were all donating some clothing items and climbing gear. But most satisfied clients did exactly that, only to be long forgotten by the time the next group arrived and the next expedition was underway. I wanted to leave them with something other than just a monetary tip and fleece jacket; something more meaningful and lasting; something from the heart. But what?

During our eight-day trek, we had forged friendships with people we were unlikely to see again, but whom we shall undoubtedly remember for the rest of our lives. The Tanzanians who accompanied us were some of the friendliest and most charming people we've met anywhere. On our very last evening, we were touched when Bruce, our guide who ran the expedition like a well-oiled machine, announced that his wife was due to have a baby any day now. (A week later he e-mailed us to say that they had a baby girl they named Precious.) With some folks who spoke English we shared stories about our families, our work, and our views on different issues ranging from the social to the political; with others we conversed in the age-old language of signs, gestures, smiles, and touch.

The cry of an augur buzzard unsettled the white-necked ravens, and one by one those black ink blots disappeared. It was nearly time for breakfast. Outside, I could hear the bustle of campers waking up and the chatter of cooks and porters making breakfast preparations. The clanking sound of pots and pans reminded me of my *pole pole* beat and the song I'd composed on our descent the day before. That's when I had the idea of sharing my piece of music with everyone at the farewell ceremony. "Perhaps I could teach everyone—my colleagues, the guides, the porters—the lyrics and we could all sing it together," I thought. I hesitated at first: "Who am I to teach Tanzanians a Swahili song when I don't even speak the language?" When Hildi woke up, I told her my idea and shared the melody of my song, which she really liked. She encouraged me to go for it and agreed that it would be fun for everyone. So I dropped my original farewell speech idea, opened my notebook to the page where I'd written the lyrics the day before, and started repeating the Swahili words and phrases in order to memorize them well. I didn't want to make a total fool of myself in front of everyone on our last day.

After breakfast, we all gathered at the center of the campsite, in front of the green rangers' hut, to say our goodbyes before our final descent to Mweka Gate (6,496 feet/1,980 meters), where a Zara Tours Land Rover would be waiting to take us back to Moshi. Bruce— tall, lanky, and serious-looking—raised his hand and commanded everyone's attention.

Everyone obeyed instantly. He commenced with his formal speech—one he must have given dozens of times before—in which he congratulated us on our safe descent and on successfully reaching the Uhuru Peak, Africa's highest point. At the end, while everyone was still clapping for him—you could tell he enjoyed being in the spotlight—Bruce signaled his team to perform their traditional Kilimanjaro song. The crew sang and danced with smiles and gleeful energy: they put their arms around each other's shoulders, moved their upper bodies backward and forward, and thumped their feet on the ground as their faces glowed in the perfect morning sun.

Grace, warmth, and dignity were words that came to mind as I intently watched the porters' dance movements, which were infused with the beauty, tradition, and culture of Chaggaland. Their full-bodied expression—steps, leaps, thumps, turns, claps—spoke volumes about the culture and its people. I was immediately inspired. That's when I grabbed a nearby empty bucket, flipped it around, and joined them by drumming on its bottom the uplifting beats of Kilimanjaro.

The echo of the porters' Kilimanjaro song sailed down the mountain like the sound of a drum inside a cave. When they concluded their performance, it was my turn to say a few words. I asked Bruce to translate into Swahili so that everyone could understand. First, I thanked the guides and porters for their hospitality and hard work. I told them that we were honored to have been their guests and that we would always remember them. Then I said that I wanted to share with them a song I wrote on the descent from the mountain, hoping to leave them with something they could remember us by. I warned them that it was a work in progress and I explained that I wanted us all to sing it together. They laughed. I reassured them that it was not difficult to learn because the song I wrote was in fact in Swahili and that in it I used all the Swahili words and phrases I learned from them over the past few days. They laughed even harder.

I wanted everyone to get a feel for the music so I started playing the beat on the yellow plastic bucket. It took only a second for everyone to get into the groove. As I drummed, my colleagues clapped in unison, and the guides and porters spontaneously improvised their African dance to my rhythm. They pounded their feet giddily and did turns; some even went down on their knees until they almost touched the ground. It was fun to watch.

I nervously introduced some lyrics by starting with the word everyone knew all too well: *pole pole* (slowly). I had everyone join me by singing the word *pole pole* at the beginning of every fourth beat. We did that four times. Then I added two more words: *pole pole, jambo jambo*. Again, four times. Then I introduced the whole phrase: *pole pole, jambo jambo, pole pole, jambo jambo*. We were jammin'. Other campers heard us singing and stopped whatever they were doing and came to watch. I was ecstatic. At that moment, I felt like an inspired follower rather than a leader.

By now everyone had got it. So I introduced the rest of the Swahili lyrics I had prepared. I divided the crowd into three groups: my colleagues were instructed to sing the refrain; the guides, assistant guides, and cook would do the call; and the porters would follow with the response. I conducted the piece amid much laughter about my choice of words: *Habari yaku* (How are you?) was the first call, to which the porters responded *Nzuri sana* (I'm fine, thank you); *Kichwa kinauma* (my head is aching) was another, to which they answered *Twende sasa* (Let's go now); *Nimechoka* (I'm tired), to which the response was *Lala salama* (Good night); and so on. This went on until I used up all the creative output of Swahili vocabulary stored in my chest. All except one word, which I used at the very end of the song together with the names of each and every member of our expedition team: *Tunakupenda* (We love you).

With this, the farewell ceremony came to an end. It was a blast! We said *kwa heri* (goodbye) and *asante sana* (thank you very much), shook hands and hugged our Tanzanian friends. We then quickly packed up our belongings and hit the trail down to Mweka Gate, with some still singing *pole pole, jambo jambo, pole pole, jambo jambo*.

—

Pole Pole Song

Michel Moushabeck

It was impossible to get the farewell gathering out of my mind. I was thinking about it the entire nine-mile (14.5-kilometer) hike down from the camp to the base of the mountain.

We started our walk at around 9:00 AM in a single file, on a very muddy trail, through a landscape drastically different from that of the upper slopes. At nearly 9,200 feet (2,800 meters) we entered a lush forest filled with bird life, age-old trees, fiery yellow and red flowers, and moss galore. The morning sun was harsh, causing my shirt to stick to my body like glue. But the vivid colors the sun rays produced in the rainforest, as they seeped through its canopy like spot lights in a theater, were uplifting. And so was the smell of the earth—not the dusty, dry smell of the lifeless desert, but sweet and pleasingly aromatic.

On the trail, my feet often sank deep in the mud; twice I lost my balance and slipped, ending up flat on my back and covered in mud from my shoulders down to my boots. When I fell the first time, a passing porter I did not recognize—he was from another group— stopped and offered me a hand. He then surprised me by saying "I like your song" and started singing it as he continued down the trail. I was equally touched when a guide from the group with the yellow tents stopped abruptly when he saw me on the trail and said in perfect English: "I want to shake your hand. You drum like an African. I will always remember you; I will always remember your song."

After this moving encounter, I was overcome with a deep sense of sadness that our journey was nearly over. A few minutes later, though, I found myself laughing when we passed a group of potbellied colobus monkeys sitting on tree branches like a bunch of bored high-school kids hanging about outside their local mall. Towards the end of trail, as we got close to the gate, we came across several hardworking, colorfully attired women cutting firewood from debris piled up on the sides. As we passed them, their young children greeted us by yelling *jambo* and then asked for candy.

We finally reached the Mweka Gate (6,496ft/1,980m) in mid-afternoon. After registering with the park ranger, we boarded the Zara Tours Land Rover and headed back to our hotel in Moshi. On the narrow, muddy, and hugely potholed dirt road the Land Rover slid

Previous pages: Montane forest/Mweka route; Above: Colobus monkeys

and lurched from side to side like a sailboat caught in a violent storm. But at that point my mind was focused on one thing and one thing only: the shower.

—

Our aim with this book was to give you a glimpse of the unimaginable journey and special world you'll find yourself part of when you venture up the vast mountain. We hope that it will inspire you to travel to Tanzania and experience the untamed beauty of Kilimanjaro for yourself. On your climb, please remember to practice "zero impact" hiking to help preserve the mountain for future generations. Whether you make it to the top or not, you are guaranteed unique encounters and breathtaking scenery on its out-of-this-world terrain that will leave you with everlasting memories.

So get your hiking gear ready—and prepare to sing *pole pole, jambo jambo.*

Porters and guides dancing at the farewell ceremony

FURTHER READING

General

Amin, Mohamed, Duncan Willetts, and John Eames. *The Last of the Maasai*. Nairobi: Camerapix Publishers, 1987.

Hemingway, Ernest. *The Snows of Kilimanjaro and Other Stories* (the short story was originally published in *Esquire* magazine in 1936). New York: Scribner Classics, 1961.

Jafferj, Jared, and Graham Mercer. *Tanzania: African Eden*. Zanzibar: The Gallery Publications, 2001.

Lithgow, Tom and Hugo van Lawick. *The Ngorongoro Story*. Nairobi: Camerapix Publishers, 2006.

Maddox, Gregory, and James L. Giblin (eds.). *In Search of a Nation: Histories of Authority and Dissidence in Tanzania*. Athens, OH: Ohio University Press, 2006.

Meyer, Hans. *Across East African Glaciers: An Account of the First Ascent of Kilimanjaro*. London: George Philip & Son, 1891.

Pluth, David, Mohamed Amin, and Graham Mercer. *Kilimanjaro: The Great White Mountain of Africa* (second ed.). Nairobi: Camerapix Publishers, 2006.

Willetts, Duncan, and John Dawson. *East Africa Alive*. Nairobi: Camerapix Publishers, 2004.

Travel, Wildlife and Climbing Guides

Allen, David J. *A Traveller's Guide to the Wildflowers and Common Trees of East Africa*. Nairobi: Camerapix Publishers, 2009.

Amin, Mohamed. *Spectrum Guide to Tanzania* (second ed.). Northampton, MA: Interlink Books, 2002.

Malik, Nasor. *The Rough Guide Phrasebook: Swahili*. London: Rough Guides Ltd, 2006.

Megarry, Jacquetta. *Explore Mount Kilimanjaro: Marangu, Machame and Rongai Routes* (third ed.). Dunblane, UK: Rucksack Readers, 2005.

Megarry, Jacquetta. *Kilimanjaro: Summit of Africa*. Dunblane, UK: Rucksack Readers, 2009.

Stevenson, Terry and John Fanshawe. *Birds of East Africa*. Princeton, NJ: Princeton University Press, 2002.

Williams, Lizzie. *Tanzania Handbook* (second ed.). Bath: Footprint Handbooks, 2009.

Maps

Kilimanjaro National Park Tourist Map and Guide (ISBN 978-3-927468-29-0, harms-ic-verlag, www.harms-ic-verlag.de) is a 1:100,000 multilingual map that includes a 1:50,000 map of Kibo, Arusha city map, Moshi city map, and all the climbing routes.

New Map of the Kilimanjaro National Park (Maco Editions, LLC, www.gtmaps.com) is a 1:125,000 map hand drawn by Giovanni Tombazzi. It shows all the climbing routes and has a useful section on the mountain's flora.

Websites

www.rucsacs.com gives background climbing information and links to selected sites, including full moon dates, ascent diaries, and tour operators' websites.

www.zaratours.com is the website of Moshi-based Zara Tanzania Adventures, a leading Kilimanjaro outfitter and safari operator. Zara is also owner of Springlands Hotel.

www.7summits.com is an independent outfitter owned and operated by Harry Kikstra, climber, expedition leader and author of several climbing guides. It offers tailor-made trips of the highest standards.